LONGEST BEARD

Hans Langseth, from Norway, is buried in Kensett, Iowa—well, most of him is. His 17-foot, 6-inch beard, which is considered the longest in the world, is proudly displayed in the Smithsonian. For more cool facts, read on!

Louise Rozett, Editor
Allicette Torres, Art Director
The Design Lab, Book Design

Library of Congress Cataloging-in-Publication Data
Fast facts about the 50 states.
    p. cm. — (America the beautiful, third series)
  Includes index.
  ISBN 978-0-531-24700-6; 0-531-24700-7
  1. U.S. states—Miscellanea—Juvenile literature. 2. United States—Miscellanea—Juvenile
literature. I. Title: Fast facts about the fifty states. II. Series.
  E180.F37 2009
  973–dc22   2009002048

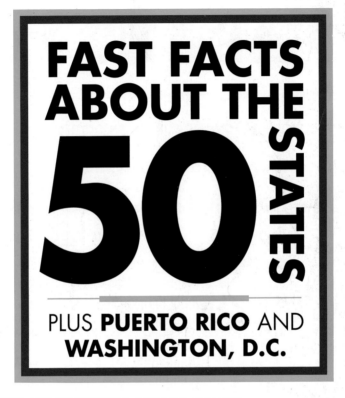

FAST FACTS ABOUT THE 50 STATES

PLUS **PUERTO RICO** AND **WASHINGTON, D.C.**

Children's Press®
An Imprint of Scholastic Inc.
New York ★ Toronto ★ London ★ Auckland ★ Sydney
Mexico City ★ New Delhi ★ Hong Kong
Danbury, Connecticut

THINGS YOU
ABOUT YOUR

The following is a partial list of things YOU
should know about your country:

★ **Superman lives in Illinois.**

★ **Burros in Arizona celebrate the
4th of July by eating eggs that fry
on the sizzling streets.**

★ **If you love green Jell-O, you
should live in Utah; if you love
chocolate Kisses or soft pretzels,
you should live in Pennsylvania.**

★ **The Etch A Sketch was
born in Ohio.**

SHOULD KNOW COUNTRY

So how do we know all this?

Here's how: We held a contest, asking a bunch of Super Smarties (aka librarians) to tell us the coolest, wackiest, and wildest facts about their states. Before we knew it, hundreds of librarians from coast to coast had sent us AMAZING facts about their states.

After a lot of teeth gnashing and hair pulling (hey, it was hard!), we picked ten—and ONLY ten—incredible facts about each state from all the entries. You are now holding the result in your hands!

Read on and enjoy, trivia and history fans!

TRUTH – JUSTICE – THE AMERICAN WAY

CONTENTS

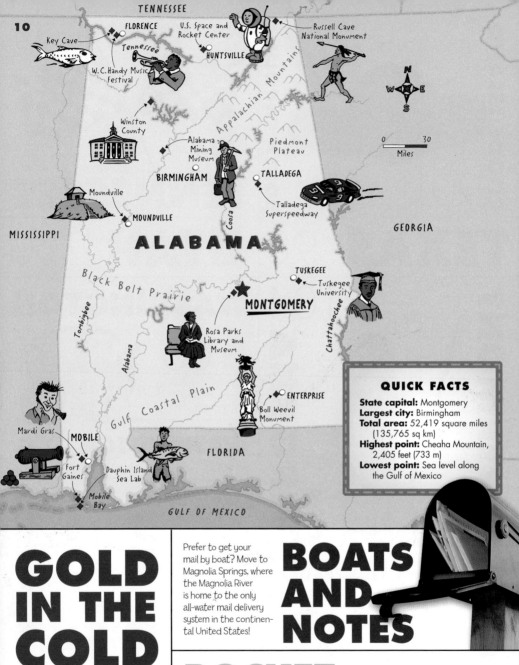

TENNESSEE

FLORENCE

Key Cave

U.S. Space and Rocket Center

Russell Cave National Monument

Tennessee

HUNTSVILLE

W.C. Handy Music Festival

Appalachian Mountains

Winston County

Alabama Mining Museum

Piedmont Plateau

BIRMINGHAM

TALLADEGA

Moundville

Talladega Superspeedway

MOUNDVILLE

Coosa

MISSISSIPPI

GEORGIA

ALABAMA

TUSKEGEE

Tuskegee University

MONTGOMERY

Black Belt Prairie

Rosa Parks Library and Museum

Tombigbee

Chattahoochee

Alabama

Gulf Coastal Plain

ENTERPRISE

Boll Weevil Monument

Mardi Gras

MOBILE

Fort Gaines

Dauphin Island Sea Lab

FLORIDA

Mobile Bay

GULF OF MEXICO

N W E S

0   30
Miles

QUICK FACTS

State capital: Montgomery
Largest city: Birmingham
Total area: 52,419 square miles
(135,765 sq km)
Highest point: Cheaha Mountain,
2,405 feet (733 m)
Lowest point: Sea level along
the Gulf of Mexico

GOLD IN THE COLD

In February 2002, Birmingham-born bobsledder Vonetta Flowers became the first person from Alabama—and the first person of African descent—to win gold in a Winter Olympics.

Prefer to get your mail by boat? Move to Magnolia Springs, where the Magnolia River is home to the only all-water mail delivery system in the continental United States!

BOATS AND NOTES

ROCKET MAN

At NASA's Marshall Space Flight Center in Huntsville, German scientist Wernher von Braun developed the rockets that sent American astronauts to the moon in 1969! How's that for flying high?

ROSA ROCKS

When civil rights activist Rosa Parks refused a bus driver's order to give up her seat to a white man in Montgomery in 1955, she ignited the civil rights movement and rocked America. Thanks, Rosa!

THE BIG SIT

The country's largest office chair stands a proud 31-feet tall in Anniston. It's made of 10 tons of steel and can withstand winds up to 85 miles per hour!

HANKIE SONGS

Need a good cry? Just listen to some Hank Williams! The legendary crooner from Alabama is famous for tearjerkers like "Your Cheatin' Heart" and "I'm So Lonesome I Could Cry."

IT'S OUTTA HERE!

Despite racist hate mail and death threats, Mobile's Hank Aaron shattered Babe Ruth's homerun record when he knocked his 715th homer out of the park on April 8, 1974.

GOING FOR THE GOLD

At the 1936 Olympic games, African American athlete Jesse Owens won four gold medals. He was not honored by an American president until 1955.

HEADS UP!

In 1954, Ann Hodges was just minding her own business on her couch in Oak Grove when an 8.5 pound meteorite smashed through her roof and landed on her! Ouch!

HELP!

On February 16, 1968, the first 911 call was made in Haleyville. The bright red phone that received that first call is now retired and living in a Haleyville museum.

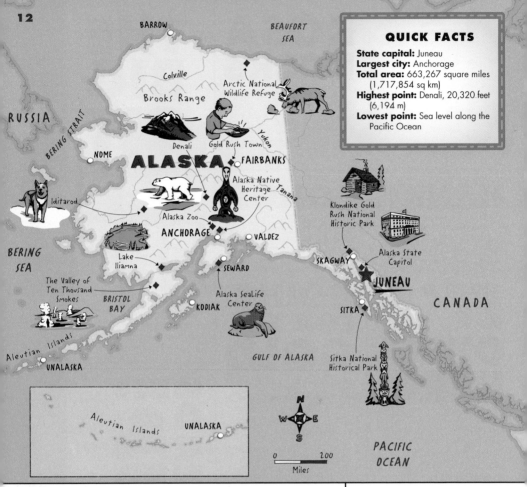

BARROW

BEAUFORT SEA

Colville

Arctic National Wildlife Refuge

Brooks Range

RUSSIA

BERING STRAIT

Denali

Gold Rush Town

Yukon

NOME

ALASKA

FAIRBANKS

Iditarod

Tanana

Alaska Native Heritage Center

Alaska Zoo

ANCHORAGE

VALDEZ

Klondike Gold Rush National Historic Park

Alaska State Capitol

BERING SEA

Lake Iliamna

SEWARD

SKAGWAY

JUNEAU

The Valley of Ten Thousand Smokes

BRISTOL BAY

KODIAK

Alaska SeaLife Center

SITKA

CANADA

Aleutian Islands

UNALASKA

GULF OF ALASKA

Sitka National Historical Park

PACIFIC OCEAN

Aleutian Islands   UNALASKA

N W E S

0   200
Miles

QUICK FACTS

State capital: Juneau
Largest city: Anchorage
Total area: 663,267 square miles (1,717,854 sq km)
Highest point: Denali, 20,320 feet (6,194 m)
Lowest point: Sea level along the Pacific Ocean

SUPERSIZED STATE

Alaska is one big state! In fact, you could fit 1/5th of the combined "Lower 48" states inside its borders. (But it's probably better for everyone if you don't!)

HUNGRY HUNTERS

Hungry in Alaska? Go fish! Alaskans are allowed to hunt more fish and game than residents in other states because grocery stores are super scarce.

The Iditarod is a musher's marathon. The course is 1,150 freezing-cold miles from Anchorage to Nome, and it took the current record holder nearly ten days to finish! BRRRR!

MUSHING MARATHON

OIL ON THE MOVE

The Trans-Alaska Pipeline is 800 miles long, 48 inches in diameter, and has been moving oil through three mountain ranges and under 800 rivers and streams since 1977. That's some pipe!

MIDNIGHT SUN

In Barrow, Alaska, the sun stays up for 24 hours on the first day of summer. And on the first day of winter, it doesn't bother to rise at all!

SHAKING AND QUAKING

The most powerful earthquake recorded in North America occurred in Anchorage on Good Friday in 1964. Effects of the quake were observed as far away as Louisiana and South Africa!

WHAT'S FOR DESSERT?!

If you're not a Native Alaskan, Eskimo Ice Cream might scare you. Its ingredients can include fish liver, reindeer fat, and seal oil. Hey—don't knock it until you try it!

DEAR SANTA...

Ever mailed a letter to Santa? It probably ended up in North Pole, Alaska. The town receives—and answers!—mail from all over the world for the jolly fellow.

EAST MEETS WEST

Both the easternmost and westernmost points of the United States are in Alaska. How can that be? Alaska straddles the 180th Meridian, the global dividing line between all eastern and western longitudes.

ICE LAND!

Five percent of Alaska is covered by glaciers—hanging glaciers, tidewater glaciers, freshwater glaciers, valley glaciers, receding glaciers. . . . You name the glacier, Alaska probably has it!

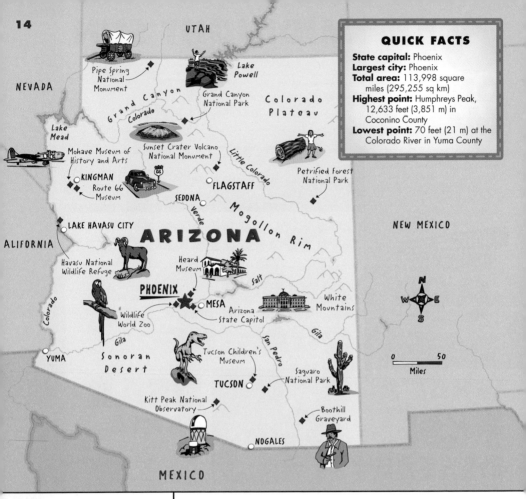

UTAH

NEVADA

Pipe Spring National Monument

Lake Powell

Grand Canyon National Park

Grand Canyon

Colorado

Colorado Plateau

Lake Mead

Mohave Museum of History and Arts

Little Colorado

Sunset Crater Volcano National Monument

Petrified Forest National Park

KINGMAN Route 66 Museum

FLAGSTAFF

SEDONA

Verde

Mogollon Rim

NEW MEXICO

LAKE HAVASU CITY

ARIZONA

CALIFORNIA

Havasu National Wildlife Refuge

Heard Museum

Salt

PHOENIX

White Mountains

Wildlife World Zoo

MESA

Arizona State Capitol

Colorado

Gila

Gila

YUMA

Sonoran Desert

Tucson Children's Museum

San Pedro

Saguaro National Park

TUCSON

Kitt Peak National Observatory

Boothill Graveyard

NOGALES

MEXICO

QUICK FACTS

State capital: Phoenix
Largest city: Phoenix
Total area: 113,998 square miles (295,255 sq km)
Highest point: Humphreys Peak, 12,633 feet (3,851 m) in Coconino County
Lowest point: 70 feet (21 m) at the Colorado River in Yuma County

0   50
Miles

ALI'S CAMEL CORPS

Syrian-born Hadji Ali helped U.S. soldiers learn to ride camels imported to build a route through the desert in the 1850s. A monument at Ali's grave in Quartzsite recognizes his service.

FROM COWS TO CASES

Sandra Day O'Connor, who became the first woman nominated to the Supreme Court in 1981, grew up on a cattle ranch in Duncan. From lassos to the law!

SUNGAZING

Kitt Peak is home to the largest solar telescope in the world. The Nicholas U. Mayall Telescope building is 187 feet tall and can be seen from 50 miles away!

LAW AND ORDER

On October 26, 1881, the famous gunfight at the O.K. Corral took place between outlaws and law officers. Wish you'd been there? Experience the showdown firsthand in Tombstone—it's reenacted daily!

OLD AS THE HILLS

Oraibi, believed to be America's oldest continuously inhabited settlement, was founded in what is now Navajo County around 1100 c.e. Go check it out but don't bother with your camera—residents don't allow photos.

SIDEWALK SNACKS

Oatman is so hot that the town hosts an egg-frying contest on its sidewalks every July 4th. But beware, contestants! Wild burros roam the town, trying to eat the entries.

GRAND GUESTS

The Grand Canyon had 44,173 visitors during its first year as a National Park in 1919. These days, it welcomes 5 million people a year from all over the world.

THE COPPER STATE

The dome of Arizona's capitol building is covered with enough copper to make 4.8 million pennies. (For you math and money fans, that's $48,000. Yowza!)

How's this for a unique contribution? The Navajo helped America win World War II by developing a code based on their complex language that no one could crack.

CRACK THIS!

BRIDGE BUY

In 1968, an Arizona businessman bought London Bridge from the British government—and had it shipped to America! The bridge was reconstructed in Lake Havasu and opened in 1971.

MISSOURI

N W E S

0   40
Miles

Arkansas Air Museum and Visitor Center

Beaver Lake

Bull Shoals Lake

Ozark Plateau

Norfork Lake

Wolf House

FAYETTEVILLE

Blanchard Springs Caverns

Black

JONESBORO

St. Francis

Mississippi

TENNESSEE

Fort Smith National Historic Site

Boston Mountains

Cedar Falls

FORT SMITH

Lake Dardanelle

USS

WEST MEMPHIS

Arkansas Inland Maritime Museum

ARKANSAS

OKLAHOMA

Fourche Lafave

Ouachita Mountains

LITTLE ROCK

Delta Cultural Center

White

MISSISSIPPI

Lake Ouachita

HOT SPRINGS

Old State House Museum

Hot Springs National Park

White River National Wildlife Refuge

Ka-Do-Ha Indian Village

MURFREESBORO

Crater of Diamonds State Park

PINE BLUFF

Arkansas

Saline

Toltec Mounds Archeological State Park

Red

TEXARKANA

Watermelon Festival

Ouachita

Mississippi

Photographer's Island

TEXARKANA TEX. ARK.

EL DORADO

TEXAS

LOUISIANA

QUICK FACTS

State capital: Little Rock
Largest city: Little Rock
Total area: 53,180 square miles (137,736 sq km)
Highest point: Magazine Mountain, 2,753 feet (839 m) in Logan County
Lowest point: 55 feet (17 m), where the Ouachita River flows from Arkansas into Louisiana

DIGGING FOR DIAMONDS

Feeling lucky? Try diamond hunting at the Crater of Diamonds State Park in Murfreesboro. You can keep whatever you find—no matter how big!

AMERICA'S SPA

Hot Springs National Park, known as "America's Spa," is home to. . . you guessed it! Hot springs! Every day, 700,000 gallons of 143° F water flows from the earth into the thermal springs.

The 1862 Battle of Pea Ridge was one of the only Civil War battles in which Native Americans participated. They fought as two Confederate regiments.

CHEROKEE CONFEDERATES

THE ARKANSAS TOOTHPICK

Before you use an Arkansas toothpick, you should know something—it's no toothpick. It's actually a dagger with a 25-inch blade. Probably best not to pick your teeth with it.

MAN IN BLACK

The legendary Johnny Cash, winner of 13 Grammy Awards and an inductee into two different halls of fame, was born in Kingsland and homegrown in Dyess.

Think your pet toad is a champion? Hop on over to Conway for the Toad Suck Daze Festival and enter your athletic amphibian in the World Championship Toad Races!

TOADALLY AWESOME!

In the winter of 1982-1983, the Griggs family of Benton hit archaeological pay dirt when they found a 300-year-old, 24-foot Indian canoe while cleaning up after the Saline River flooded their farm.

CULTURAL CANOE

HOME OF THE BRAVE

In 1957, nine African American students—known as the Little Rock Nine—attended the previously all-white Central High School in Little Rock, taking one brave, giant step for humankind.

LIGHTS, CAMERA, ACTION!

The Legend of Boggy Creek is a film about the Fouke Monster, a hairy, red-eyed "cryptid" who started haunting Arkansas residents in 1946. Real? Imaginary? You be the judge . . .

IDENTITY CRISIS

The South Arkansas Vine-Ripe Pink Tomato is the state fruit—and vegetable—of Arkansas. The tomato is considered a fruit but often used as a vegetable, so why not call it both?!

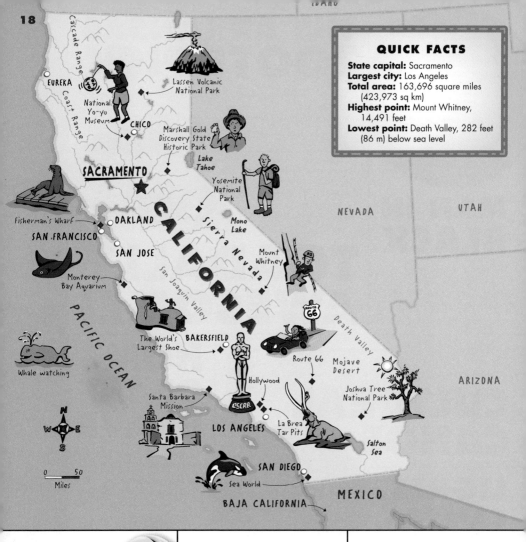

IDAHO

CASCADE Range

Coast Range

EUREKA

National
Yo-yo
Museum

CHICO

Lassen Volcanic
National Park

Marshall Gold
Discovery State
Historic Park

Lake
Tahoe

Yosemite
National
Park

SACRAMENTO

CALIFORNIA

Fisherman's Wharf

OAKLAND

Mono
Lake

SAN FRANCISCO

SAN JOSE

Sierra Nevada

Mount
Whitney

Monterey
Bay Aquarium

San Joaquin Valley

Whale watching

PACIFIC OCEAN

The World's
Largest Shoe

BAKERSFIELD

ROUTE
66

Death Valley

Route 66

Mojave
Desert

Hollywood

OSCAR

Santa Barbara
Mission

Joshua Tree
National Park

ARIZONA

N
W E
S

LOS ANGELES

La Brea
Tar Pits

Salton
Sea

0   50
Miles

SAN DIEGO

Sea World

MEXICO

BAJA CALIFORNIA

NEVADA   UTAH

QUICK FACTS

State capital: Sacramento
Largest city: Los Angeles
Total area: 163,696 square miles
(423,973 sq km)
Highest point: Mount Whitney,
14,491 feet
Lowest point: Death Valley, 282 feet
(86 m) below sea level

YO! YO-YOs!

In 1928, Pedro Flores started a national yo-yo craze when he made his dream of mass-producing the toy a reality and opened a factory in Santa Barbara.

TREE IN HIDING

The oldest tree in North America is believed to be in Bishop—in the Ancient Bristle Cone Pine Forest—but the exact location of the 4,600-year-old tree is kept secret, to protect it.

Do you know how many earthquakes and tremors are recorded in California each year? About half a million! Stay safe, Californians—secure those bookcases and put latches on your cabinets.

SHAKE, RATTLE, & ROLL

CABLE-ICIOUS!

The two main cables of San Francisco's Golden Gate Bridge contain 80,000 miles of steel wire. That's enough to circle the equator over three times!

FLYING RICE

Want to be a California rice farmer? Get your pilot's license. In the Golden State, rice is planted from the air, by planes flying at 100 miles per hour!

MOBILE MONUMENT

If you like to keep moving when you sightsee, head to San Francisco and check out America's only mobile national monument—the cable car. Hop on and get some history!

TALL TEMPERATURES

Baker hosts the World's Largest Thermometer. It's 134 feet tall, in honor of the hottest day in U.S. history—134 degrees in 1913, in nearby Death Valley. Sizzling!

CHEWY WALLS

Need somewhere to put your gum? Visit Bubble Gum Alley in San Luis Obispo, and stick it on the wall alongside more pieces of gum than anyone would ever want to count.

HIGHS AND LOWS

California has both the highest and the lowest points in the Lower 48. Weird, right? The difference between Mount Whitney (14,491 feet above sea level) and Death Valley (282 feet below sea level) is 14,773 feet!

Live in California? You'd better like nuts! The Golden State produces most of the country's walnuts and almonds, thanks to places like Fresno, one of California's top agricultural counties.

GOING NUTS

CALIFORNIA THE GOLDEN STATE

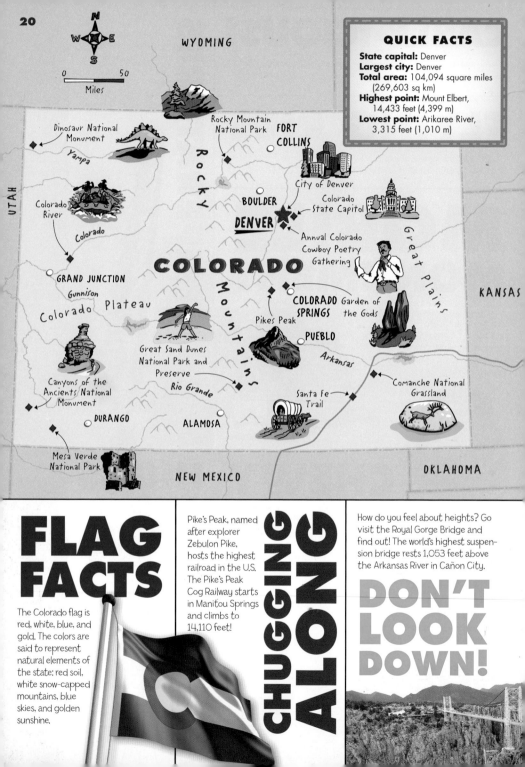

N W E S

0 50
Miles

WYOMING

Dinosaur National Monument

Yampa

Rocky Mountain National Park

FORT COLLINS

City of Denver

Colorado River

Colorado

BOULDER

DENVER

Colorado State Capitol

Annual Colorado Cowboy Poetry Gathering

COLORADO

Great Plains

GRAND JUNCTION

Gunnison

Colorado Plateau

Mountains

Pikes Peak

COLORADO SPRINGS

Garden of the Gods

PUEBLO

Arkansas

Great Sand Dunes National Park and Preserve

Rio Grande

Canyons of the Ancients National Monument

Santa Fe Trail

Comanche National Grassland

DURANGO

ALAMOSA

Mesa Verde National Park

NEW MEXICO

OKLAHOMA

KANSAS

UTAH

QUICK FACTS

State capital: Denver
Largest city: Denver
Total area: 104,094 square miles (269,603 sq km)
Highest point: Mount Elbert, 14,433 feet (4,399 m)
Lowest point: Arikaree River, 3,315 feet (1,010 m)

FLAG FACTS

The Colorado flag is red, white, blue, and gold. The colors are said to represent natural elements of the state: red soil, white snow-capped mountains, blue skies, and golden sunshine.

CHUGGING ALONG

Pike's Peak, named after explorer Zebulon Pike, hosts the highest railroad in the U.S. The Pike's Peak Cog Railway starts in Manitou Springs and climbs to 14,110 feet!

How do you feel about heights? Go visit the Royal Gorge Bridge and find out! The world's highest suspension bridge rests 1,053 feet above the Arkansas River in Cañon City.

DON'T LOOK DOWN!

THE HIGH LIFE

ENDLESS AVENUE

The longest continuous street in America is Denver's Colfax Avenue. The 40-mile-long street has many claims to fame, including several mentions in Jack Kerouac's novel *On the Road*.

OSCAR HISTORY

Hattie McDaniel, the first African American to win an Oscar, grew up in Denver. The singer and actress appeared in over 300 films, receiving credit for only about 90.

DONKEY DASH

At the end of July in Fairplay, competitors in the Burro Days' 29-mile race must dash from downtown Fairplay to the summit of Mosquito Pass—while leading a donkey.

About 1,000 years ago, ancestors of the Anasazi people built houses into the cliffs in what is now Mesa Verde National Park. There was no rolling out of bed in those houses!

THE FOUR CORNERS

U.S. DEPARTMENT OF THE INTERIOR
UTAH | COLORADO
ARIZONA | NEW MEXICO
CADASTRAL SURVEY
BUREAU OF LAND MANAGEMENT
1922

Can't decide where to go? Cover all your bases and head to Colorado's southwest corner where you can stand in Arizona, New Mexico, Utah, and Colorado at the same time!

Activist Margaret Brown, who lived for a time in Leadville, became known posthumously as the Unsinkable Molly Brown, a reference to having survived the sinking of the *Titanic* in 1912.

UNSINKABLE, INDEED!

CAR-PART CRITTERS

The Swetsville Zoo in Timnath was home to over 160 scrap-metal creatures including a giant car with spider legs and dinosaur-like monsters rocking out in a "heavy metal" band.

QUICK FACTS

State capital: Hartford
Largest city: Bridgeport
Total area: 5,543 square miles
(14,356 sq km)
Highest point: Mount Frissell,
2,380 feet (725 m)
Lowest point: Sea level at Long
Island Sound

Mount Frissell

MASSACHUSETTS

Litchfield Hills

Appalachian
Trail

Taconic Mountains

Shenipsit
Lake

State Capitol

HARTFORD

Bantam
Lake

RHODE
ISLAND

NEW
YORK

Dinosaur State Park

CONNECTICUT

Housatonic

Lake
Candlewood

Railroad Museum of
New England

WATERBURY

Lake
Pocotopaug

Gardner Lake

Old
Lighthouse
Museum

Connecticut

Connecticut River

Naugatuck

Yale University

NEW LONDON

Thames

Barnum
Museum

NEW HAVEN

BRIDGEPORT

Mystic
Seaport

STAMFORD

Long Island
Sound

Long Island Sound

WHAT'S IN A NAME?

If you were trying to name a town that was halfway between Hartford and New Haven, what would you name it? Hmm, that's a tough one. How about . . . Middletown?!

GENIUS INVENTION!

A father and semi-pro pitcher from Fairfield invented Wiffle Ball for his son, whose arm hurt from trying to prevent broken windows by throwing a golf ball instead of a baseball.

T.KEELER's INN

SEEING IS BELIEVING

Looking for tangible evidence of the Revolutionary War? Go to the Keeler Tavern Museum in Ridgefield, where a British cannonball is still lodged in one of the tavern's beams!

BIG! HUGE! JUMBO?

Circus showman P.T. Barnum of Bethel introduced the word "jumbo" into American English when he imported a supersized elephant named Jumbo from London in 1882.

DINOSAUR DISCOVERY

Rocky Hill is home to 2,000 dinosaur footprints. Workers excavating a site for a new building found the 200-million-year-old tracks by accident! Now the site is a Registered Natural Landmark.

In 1687, as British officials argued with Connecticut lawmakers over the colony's charter, Captain Joseph Wadsworth grabbed the document and hid it in an oak tree for safekeeping.

THE CHARTER OAK

SAY WHAT?

In 1806, Thomas Jefferson sued *The Hartford Courant* for libel when the paper wrote that Jefferson bribed French officials to win their support. Jefferson lost the case in the Supreme Court.

B-BALL FOR ALL

The University of Connecticut is the first state university to have both its men's and women's basketball teams win NCAA championships in the same year. Go, Huskies!

BILLIONS OF PEZ

Americans love their PEZ—they eat 3 billion of the sweet treats a year! Manufactured in Orange, PEZ is as famous for its dispensers as for its sugary taste.

WORDSMITH WEBSTER

Next time you look up a word, think of smarty-pants Noah Webster from Hartford, author of the first American dictionary, published in 1828. (How did he know all those words?!)

CONNECTICUT

THE CONSTITUTION STATE

Winterthur Museum and Country Estate

PENNSYLVANIA

WILMINGTON

Delaware Art Museum

NEWARK
Iron Hill Museum

Christina

NEW CASTLE

Fort Delaware State Park

Chesapeake and Delaware Canal

Chesapeake Bay

NEW JERSEY

SMYRNA

Delaware

Leipsic

DOVER

Delaware State House

Bombay Hook National Wildlife Refuge

St. Jones

Atlantic

Delaware Bay

Coastal Plain

MARYLAND

MILFORD

PRIMEHOOK BEACH

DELAWARE

Cape Henlepen State Park

LEWES

ATLANTIC OCEAN

Nanticoke Indian Museum

SEAFORD

Nanticoke

MILLSBORO

Indian

Rehoboth Bay

Boardwalk at Rehoboth Beach

Indian River Bay

Cypress Swamp

DiscoverSea Shipwreck Museum

MARYLAND

N W E S

0   10
Miles

QUICK FACTS

State capital: Dover
Largest city: Wilmington
Total area: 2,489 square miles (6,446 sq km)
Highest point: 451 feet (137 m), in New Castle County along the Pennsylvania state line
Lowest point: Sea level, along the coast

WATER POWER

The famous American chemical company DuPont had modest beginnings in 1802 as a gunpowder factory powered by the steep drop in elevation of the Brandywine River.

#1 STATE

Delaware, the "First State," was the first of the original thirteen colonies to ratify the U.S. Constitution. Ratification took place in 1787 at Dover's Golden Fleece Tavern.

A GOOD CITIZEN

Thomas Garrett, a Quaker iron merchant from Wilmington, lost everything when a court fined him for helping 2,000 slaves to freedom on the Underground Railroad. He continued his work anyway.

MONSTER MONUMENT

The 46-foot-tall Miles the Monster at the Dover International Speedway is one of the tallest fiberglass structures anywhere. He even has a full-sized stock car in one hand!

FIT FOR A QUEEN

The Christina River, named after a queen of Sweden, has had more than 25 names over the years, including Christeen Creek, Christiany River, Minquaas Kill, and Sickpeckons.

SQUISHED SQUASH!

Every year around Halloween, people gather in Bridgeville and use catapults and other machines to fling pumpkins far and wide—the record is 3,000 feet!—in the World Championship Punkin' Chunkin'.

LET'S SPLIT IT!

Delmar is known as "the little town too big for one state"—it's in both Delaware and Maryland (hence the name). The state line runs right down the center of town!

FOR REAL?

Delaware has exactly zero acres of land run by the National Park Service. (The national parks along the Delaware River are in New Jersey, New York, and Pennsylvania.)

BATTLE FOR THE BRIDGE

The Battle of Cooch's Bridge was the only Revolutionary War battle fought in Delaware. Legend has it that the 13-star flag was flown for the first time in this battle.

BIG DEAL

Why would someone who lives in New Jersey, Maryland, or Pennsylvania drive all the way to Delaware just to shop? Because there's no sales tax!

ALABAMA

GEORGIA

Florida Panhandle

State Capitol

PENSACOLA

TALLAHASSEE

ATLANTIC OCEAN

St. Augustine

JACKSONVILLE

Gulf Islands National Seashore

FLORIDA

Daytona International Speedway

OCALA

UNIVERSAL

Universal Orlando

John F. Kennedy Space Center

GULF OF MEXICO

Plant City

Florida Peninsula

ORLANDO

N W E S

TAMPA

PLANT CITY

Walt Disney World/ EPCOT/ MGM Studios

ST. PETERSBURG

0   50
Miles

The John and Mable Ringling Museum of Art

SARASOTA

Bok Tower

WEST PALM BEACH

The Villa Vizcaya Museum and Gardens

Sanibel Island

MIAMI

Everglades National Park

Miami Beach

KEY WEST

Florida Keys

QUICK FACTS

State capital: Tallahassee
Largest city: Jacksonville
Total area: 65,755 square miles
(170,305 sq km)
Highest point: In Walton County,
345 feet (105 m) above sea level
Lowest point: Sea level along the
Atlantic Ocean

SOFT AND STRONG

The walls of the 17th century fort Castillo de San Marcos, in St. Augustine, were made of coquina, a type of soft limestone that could actually absorb cannonballs!

CATFISH CROSSING

Look both ways when you're crossing the road in Florida. You might catch sight of the Asian catfish *Clarias batrachus* making its way across the street. (No, we're not kidding.)

Clearwater has the highest rate of lightning strikes per capita. Clearwater residents who work outdoors in spring, summer, or fall are more likely to be struck than Americans anywhere else!

LOOK OUT!

CUSTOM MADE WEATHER

The Vehicle Assembly Building at Cape Canaveral's Kennedy Space Center has such a high ceiling that rain clouds form inside on humid days!

HAPPY NEW YEAR!

If you were in Tampa on January 1, 1914, your New Year's resolution could have been to take the first flight on the country's first commercial airline, the St. Petersburg-Tampa Airboat Line.

TANNING HISTORY

Miami Beach pharmacist Benjamin Green invented suntan lotion in 1944 by cooking cocoa butter on a stove and testing it on his head. He called it Coppertone Suntan Cream.

STORY TIME

Some of the highest paid workers in Ybor City's cigar factories never touched a cigar. They read aloud to the workers, who contributed weekly to pay the reader.

DR. ICE

It makes sense that the man who popularized ice came from one of the hottest states in the country! Dr. John Gorrie of Apalachicola patented an ice machine in 1851.

GATOR AID!

In 1965, a professor at the University of Florida in Gainesville invented Gatorade when the school's football players suffered from dehydration. Where did the name come from? Gator, the school's mascot!

The Everglades is the only place on earth where alligators and crocodiles live side by side. Does that make you want to visit—or stay far away? Hard to say . . .

CRAZY COHABITATION

TENNESSEE
NORTH CAROLINA
SOUTH CAROLINA
ALABAMA
FLORIDA
ATLANTIC OCEAN

Lookout Mountain
Blue Ridge Mountains
ROME
Etowah
ATHENS
Ty Cobb Museum
ATLANTA
Georgia State Capitol
Martin Luther King Jr. National Historic Site
Ocmulgee National Monument
MACON
AUGUSTA
Augusta National Golf Club
Savannah
Savannah River
COLUMBUS
GEORGIA
Ocmulgee
Oconee
SAVANNAH
Altamaha
ALBANY
Albany Civil Rights Movement Museum
St. Simons Island
Sea Islands
Chattahoochee
Flint
Okefenokee Swamp
Okefenokee Swamp
Cumberland Island National Seashore

N W E S

0   40
Miles

QUICK FACTS

State capital: Atlanta
Largest city: Atlanta
Total area: 59,425 square miles (153,909 sq km)
Highest point: Brasstown Bald mountain, 4,784 feet (1,458 m)
Lowest point: Sea level at the Atlantic Ocean

GOLD GREED

Cherokee Indian culture flourished in Georgia until the Georgia Gold Rush started in Dahlonega in 1829. By 1838, the Native Americans had been forced to leave their land.

HISTORIC HOSPITAL BIRTH

Peanut farmer Jimmy Carter was the first U.S. president to be born in a hospital! He was born in Plains.

SWEET Ps

Georgia is full of yummy things to snack on, and most of them start with the letter "p"! The state is among the country's top producers of peanuts, peaches, and pecans.

BIZARRE BABIES

Babyland General Hospital in Cleveland is the birthplace of all Cabbage Patch Kids. It has a maternity ward, a nursery, and a gift shop where visitors can "adopt" a doll.

Blackbeard Island is named after Edward "Blackbeard" Teach, a legendary pirate who is rumored to have buried his treasure on the island. His loot remains to be found, treasure hunters!

BURIED TREASURE

GRANITE GENERALS

Stone Mountain is the world's largest mass of exposed granite, making it the ideal place for the world's largest high-relief sculpture! The Confederate Memorial Carving is bigger than a football field.

NAME AND RENAME

Atlanta was originally called Terminus in 1837, because the area was quickly developing around a new railroad that was going to "terminate," or end, there. (Frankly, we like "Atlanta" better.)

REUNION THROUGH SONG

An American anthropologist connected Mary Moran of Harris Neck with long-lost relatives in Sierra Leone through a song brought over by enslaved Africans and passed down through generations.

Okefenokee Swamp is about 7,000 years old, and home to over 400 species of animals! Okefenokee is a Choctaw Indian word meaning "land of the trembling earth."

WILD (LIFE) REFUGE

SODA'S STORY

In 1886, pharmacist and chemist John Stith Pemberton invented Coca-Cola in Atlanta. It was originally called Pemberton's French Wine Coca—because it had wine in it!

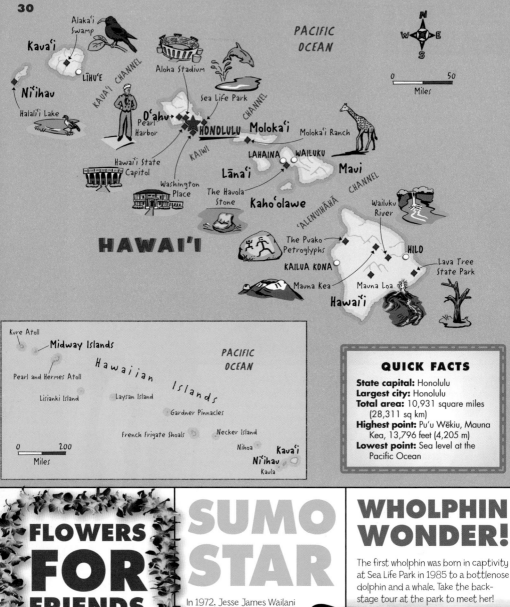

PACIFIC OCEAN

Kaua'i
Alaka'i Swamp
Ni'ihau
LĪHU'E
Halali'i Lake
KAUA'I CHANNEL
Aloha Stadium
Sea Life Park
O'ahu
Pearl Harbor
HONOLULU
KAIWI
Moloka'i
Moloka'i Ranch
LAHAINA
WAILUKU
Lāna'i
Maui
Hawai'i State Capitol
Washington Place
The Havola Stone
Kaho'olawe
'ALENUIHĀHĀ
Wailuku River
The Puako Petroglyphs
KAILUA KONA
HILO
Lava Tree State Park
Mauna Kea
Mauna Loa
Hawai'i

HAWAI'I

50 Miles

Kure Atoll
Midway Islands
Hawaiian Islands
PACIFIC OCEAN
Pearl and Hermes Atoll
Lisianki Island
Laysan Island
Gardner Pinnacles
French Frigate Shoals
Necker Island
Nihoa
Kaua'i
Ni'ihau
Kaula

0   200
Miles

QUICK FACTS

State capital: Honolulu
Largest city: Honolulu
Total area: 10,931 square miles (28,311 sq km)
Highest point: Pu'u Wēkiu, Mauna Kea, 13,796 feet (4,205 m)
Lowest point: Sea level at the Pacific Ocean

FLOWERS FOR FRIENDS

On May 1, Hawaiian friends give each other leis for Lei Day. The tradition started in the late 1920s, and even has its own song—"May Day is Lei Day in Hawai'i."

SUMO STAR

In 1972, Jesse James Wailani Kuhaulua, a former high school football player, became the first non-Japanese athlete to be a sumo champion. He competed for 20 years—unheard of in wrestling!

WHOLPHIN WONDER!

The first wholphin was born in captivity at Sea Life Park in 1985 to a bottlenose dolphin and a whale. Take the backstage tour at the park to meet her!

NO JOKE

On April Fools Day in 1946, children from Laupahoehoe reported that the ocean disappeared. People thought they were kidding, but they weren't—they were witnessing a tsunami.

LONG-TERM LAVA

Hawai'i's volcano Kilauea is the most active volcano in the world. It started erupting on January 3, 1983, and it hasn't stopped since. That's a lot of lava!

AMERICA'S PALACE

The only palace on American soil is the 'Iolani Royal Palace in Honolulu, built in 1882. It was home to the last two rulers of the Kingdom of Hawai'i.

COFFEE-LOVERS PARADISE

Hawai'i is the only place in the United States that grows coffee, producing 6 to 7 million pounds of coffee beans per year.

MACADAMIA MADNESS

Sugar plantation manager William H. Purvis brought macadamia tree seeds to Hawai'i from Australia in 1881 and unknowingly gave Hawai'i one of its most famous products!

EXTRAORDINARY ELVIS!

Rock star and soldier Elvis Presley donated over $50,000 in proceeds from his 1961 Honolulu concert to help build the USS *Arizona* War Memorial, commemorating those who died at Pearl Harbor.

DUKE OF FIRSTS

Duke Paoa Kahinu Mokoe Hulikohola Kahanamoku won an Olympic gold medal for Hawai'i in 1912 in the 100-meter freestyle. He was also America's first surfing star. Hang ten, Duke!

QUICK FACTS

State capital: Boise
Largest city: Boise
Total area: 83,570 square miles
(216,445 sq km)
Highest point: Borah Peak, 12,668
feet (3,861 m) in Custer County
Lowest point: 710 feet (216 m)
along the Snake River in Nez
Perce County

Boundary County Museum

Kootenai

COEUR D'ALENE

Hiawatha Trail

Coeur d'Alene Lake

St. Joe

WASHINGTON

Appaloosa Museum

Nez Perce National Historical Park

MONTANA

Hells Canyon

LEWISTON

Rocky Mountains

Salmon

Bitterroot National Forest

Snake

N
W   E
S

0   40
Miles

Central Idaho Historical Museum

IDAHO

OREGON

Idaho State Capitol

BOISE

Craters of the Moon National Monument

Museum of Idaho

Snake

WYOMING

IDAHO FALLS

Idaho Potato Museum

Hagerman Fossil Beds National Monument

American Falls Reservoir

POCATELLO

National Oregon/California Trail Center

Snake

TWIN FALLS

Minidoka Internment National Monument

Owyhee

Bruneau

Bear

Bear Lake

NEVADA   UTAH

IN HOT WATER

The Idaho Capitol Building is heated by hot water pumped up from 3,000 feet underground. It's the only capitol building in the nation that's warmed by a geothermal well!

HOME OF HOKEY

Legend has it that songwriter Larry LaPrise and pals wrote "The Hokey Pokey" in 1949 to entertain Sun Valley skiers. "Put your left ski in, put your left ski out . . ."

CANYON STATS

Hell's Canyon, North America's deepest river gorge, is 10 miles wide and more than 8,000 feet below He Devil Peak, the top of Idaho's Seven Devils Mountains. That's deep, all right.

HORSE HISTORY

The Hagerman Fossil Beds is home to the Hagerman Horse Quarry, the largest concentration of horse fossils in North America. Some consider it the most important horse history site in the world.

RIVERS GALORE

Idaho has 3,100 miles of rivers, which is more than any other state. So if you live in Idaho but you don't like the water, consider moving just about anywhere else!

BALANCING ACT

Balanced Rock, near Buhl, is 48-feet high, weighs 40 tons, and rests on a base that is 3 feet by 17 inches. Think twice before you sit under it!

MOON ON EARTH

In 1969, the Apollo 14 crew went to the moon without leaving the earth! How? They visited Craters of the Moon National Monument to prepare for their trip into space.

GIANT CRUNCH

Are you a potato chip fanatic? Go visit the world's largest potato chip in the Idaho Potato Museum in Blackfoot. It's 14 inches by 25 inches; that should satisfy your cravings!

IDAHO POTATO MUSEUM
BLACKFOOT IDAHO

Philo T. Farnsworth first sketched his invention—the television—for a teacher on a chalkboard at Rigby High School when he was 14 years old. How's that for precocious?

DYNAMIC DOODLE

LUCKY LEAPER

In 1974, motorcycle daredevil Evel Knievel tried to jump Snake River Canyon. The results were disastrous and Knievel crashed. However, in daredevil fashion, he walked away with only minor injuries.

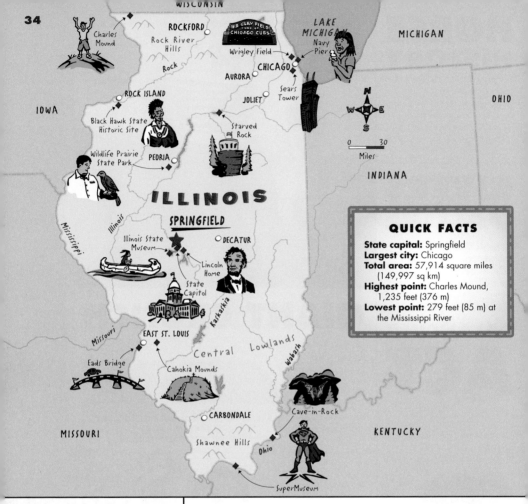

WISCONSIN

Charles Mound

ROCKFORD

Rock River Hills

Rock

WRIGLEY FIELD HOME OF THE CHICAGO CUBS

Wrigley Field

LAKE MICHIGAN

Navy Pier

MICHIGAN

CHICAGO

AURORA

Sears Tower

ROCK ISLAND

JOLIET

IOWA

OHIO

Black Hawk State Historic Site

Starved Rock

N

W   E

S

Wildlife Prairie State Park

PEORIA

0   30
Miles

INDIANA

ILLINOIS

SPRINGFIELD

DECATUR

Illinois State Museum

Lincoln Home

Mississippi

Illinois

State Capitol

Kaskaskia

Missouri

EAST ST. LOUIS

Central   Lowlands

Wabash

Eads Bridge

Cahokia Mounds

Cave-in-Rock

MISSOURI

CARBONDALE

KENTUCKY

Shawnee Hills

Ohio

SuperMuseum

QUICK FACTS

State capital: Springfield
Largest city: Chicago
Total area: 57,914 square miles
(149,997 sq km)
Highest point: Charles Mound,
1,235 feet (376 m)
Lowest point: 279 feet (85 m) at
the Mississippi River

WONDERFUL
WHEEL

The Ferris Wheel debuted at the 1893 Chicago World's Fair, designed by George Ferris of Galesburg. It was 250 feet tall and had 36 wooden cars, which each held 60 passengers!

WACKY WATER

Every year, the Chicago River magically turns emerald green on St. Patrick's Day! (Well, not quite magically—a man named Mike Butler dyes the river in honor of the holiday.)

INNOCENT
COW!

In 1871, a newspaper blamed Mrs. O'Leary's cow for kicking over the lantern that started the Great Chicago Fire, but a reporter later confessed to making up the story.

SPECTACULAR SUE!

Visit the world's largest Tyrannosaurus Rex skeleton in the Field Museum in Chicago. Her name is Sue—after the fossil hunter who found her—and she's 67 million years old!

LOOPY LAB

In 1942, Enrico Fermi built the first nuclear reactor, working in a lab that had previously been a squash court under Stagg Field, the University of Chicago's football stadium.

CATSUP CAPER

The World's Largest Catsup Bottle stands 170 feet tall in Collinsville. But don't bother visiting the bottle with your burger—it's just a water tower. Bummer!

FABULOUS FASTENER

The hookless fastener that keeps our pants up on a daily basis—aka the zipper—was invented in Chicago in 1891. Can you imagine a world without zippers? We can't, either.

Illinois has one of the highest numbers of personalized—or vanity—license plates in the nation. That's a lot of "vanitized" cars!

TRUTH — JUSTICE — THE AMERICAN WAY

ILLINOIS IS GR8!

MAKING IT UP

Before he was president, Tampico-born broadcaster Ronald Reagan improvised the events of a 1934 Chicago Cubs game for listeners when the wire that was feeding him information went dead!

SUPER OBSESSION

A 15-foot-tall, two-ton sculpture of Superman watches over Metropolis—naturally! The town proclaims itself the "Hometown of Superman" and even has a newspaper called *The Planet!*

ILLINOIS

THE PRAIRIE STATE

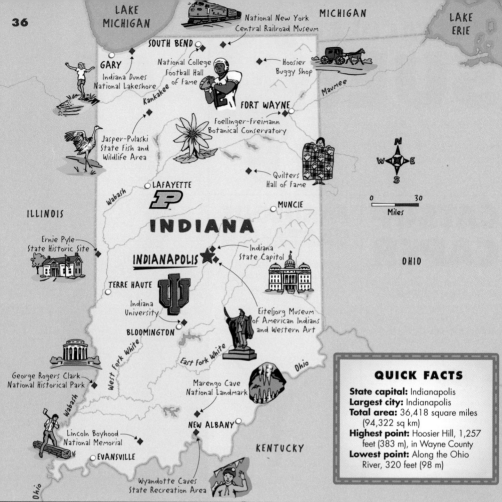

LAKE MICHIGAN

MICHIGAN

LAKE ERIE

National New York Central Railroad Museum

SOUTH BEND

GARY

Indiana Dunes National Lakeshore

Hoosier Buggy Shop

National College Football Hall of Fame

Kankakee

Maumee

FORT WAYNE

Foellinger-Freimann Botanical Conservatory

Jasper-Pulaski State Fish and Wildlife Area

Quilters Hall of Fame

N
W   E
S

LAFAYETTE

Wabash

MUNCIE

0   30
Miles

INDIANA

Ernie Pyle State Historic Site

ILLINOIS

Indiana State Capitol

OHIO

INDIANAPOLIS

TERRE HAUTE

Indiana University

Eiteljorg Museum of American Indians and Western Art

West Fork White

East Fork White

BLOOMINGTON

Ohio

George Rogers Clark National Historical Park

Marengo Cave National Landmark

Wabash

NEW ALBANY

Lincoln Boyhood National Memorial

KENTUCKY

EVANSVILLE

Ohio

Wyandotte Caves State Recreation Area

QUICK FACTS

State capital: Indianapolis
Largest city: Indianapolis
Total area: 36,418 square miles (94,322 sq km)
Highest point: Hoosier Hill, 1,257 feet (383 m), in Wayne County
Lowest point: Along the Ohio River, 320 feet (98 m)

NO PHOTOS, PLEASE!

According to published accounts, when the Secret Service stopped *Indianapolis News* photographer Paul Shideler from taking President Herbert Hoover's photo, the paper complained, and the press won the right to photograph the president.

Martinsville was home to America's first successful goldfish farm, the Grassyfork Fisheries. Within 50 years of opening in 1899, it produced 25 million fish a year!

FISH GOLD!

TORNADO TORMENT

Tornadoes have struck Indiana in every month of the year. So much for tornado season! The state sees an average of about 23 tornadoes annually.

MAKEUP
MILLIONAIRE!

Indianapolis entrepreneur and social activist Madam C.J. Walker became one of America's first female millionaires in the early 1900s by manufacturing cosmetics for black women. She started her business by going door-to-door.

TASTY
TREATS

In one year, Indiana produced more than 192.5 million pounds of popcorn and 68 million gallons of ice cream. Now THAT'S a great claim to fame!

ALL
ABOARD

The Fountain City home of Quaker abolitionists Levi and Catharine Coffin was a very busy stop on the Underground Railroad—so busy, in fact, that it was nicknamed Grand Central Station.

SPECIAL
STONE

Several of the country's most famous buildings were constructed with Indiana limestone, including the Pentagon, the Empire State Building—and the new Yankee Stadium!

TRAIN
THIEVES

The notorious Reno Gang committed the first U.S. train robbery when they jumped a train leaving Seymour and stole $12,000. (That's about $164,000 in today's economy.)

LET
THERE
BE…

Wabash became the first American city to have electric streetlamps in 1880. The cost for one year was $712, and the city council was thrilled with such "marvelous cheapness."

SECOND
TO
ONE

WELCOME TO HUNTINGTON HOME OF THE 44TH VICE PRESIDENT DAN QUAYLE

Indiana is known as the "Mother of Vice-Presidents," having produced five, including Dan Quayle, whose museum in Huntington boasts the slogan "Second to One."

INDIANA

THE HOOSIER STATE

MINNESOTA

WISCONSIN

Laura Ingalls Wilder Park and Museum

Big Sioux

Ice Cream Capital of the World

Vesterheim Norwegian-American Museum

DECORAH

Driftless Area

MASON CITY

Mississippi

SIOUX CITY

Little Sioux

Cedar

DUBUQUE

Iowa State Capitol

Iowa

WATERLOO

National Farm Toy Museum

Wapsipinicon

IOWA

CEDAR RAPIDS

Herbert Hoover National Historic Site

Missouri

DES MOINES

Devonian Fossil Gorge

DAVENPORT

DeSoto National Wildlife Refuge

Living History Farms

Pella Historical Village

Buffalo Bill Museum

COUNCIL BLUFFS

Mississippi Valley

NEBRASKA

Iowa State Fair

National Balloon Museum

Des Moines

ILLINOIS

Covered Bridges of Madison County

Airpower Museum

Snake Alley

Mississippi

MISSOURI

QUICK FACTS

State capital: Des Moines
Largest city: Des Moines
Total area: 56,272 square miles (145,744 sq km)
Highest point: Hawkeye Point at 1,670 feet (509 m), in Osceola County
Lowest point: 480 feet (146 m) along the Mississippi River, in Lee County

N
W   E
S

0   40
Miles

4-H FOUNDER

Jessie Field Shambaugh of Shenandoah started the boys and girls clubs that ultimately became the 4-H Club. She also developed the four-leaf clover design that now represents the club nationally.

Every year, the citizens of LeClaire have a tug-of-war over the Mississippi River with their neighbors in Port Byron, IL. The event requires a 2,400-foot, 680-pound rope!

HUGE HOAX

In 1862, a fossilized 10-foot-tall man was discovered in New York. People flipped out—until it was revealed that "the giant" had been carved out of gypsum from Fort Dodge.

TUG FEST

IOWA

BEST BEARD

Hans Langseth, from Norway, is buried in Kensett—well, most of him is. His 17-foot, 6-inch beard, which is considered the longest in the world, is proudly displayed in the Smithsonian.

OBELISK OF HONOR

Sioux City's 100-foot-tall obelisk commemorates Sergeant Charles Floyd, the only fatality of the nearly two-and-a-half-year-long Lewis and Clark expedition.

BUTTERY BOVINE

Butter Cow, the annual giant cow sculpture at the Iowa State Fair, is made with about 600 pounds of butter. She can provide butter for approximately 19,200 slices of toast!

BIG BERRY

The world's largest strawberry can be found in Strawberry Point, outside City Hall. It's 15 feet tall! (It's also made of fiberglass, so don't try to eat it.)

HEARTLAND ART

The 1930 painting *American Gothic* by Grant Wood of Cedar Rapids features a farmer and his daughter (and a pitchfork). The models for his painting? His sister and his dentist.

MODEST BEGINNINGS

When the Ringling brothers saw a circus being unloaded at the docks in McGregor, they decided to start their own circus—in their backyard. And the rest is history!

TRAGIC TRUMPETER

Davenport's mysterious Bix Beiderbecke was one of the best trumpet players who ever lived. The self-taught jazz musician and composer—"golden boy" to his friends—died at age 28.

NEBRASKA

IOWA

MISSOURI

N W E S

Pawnee Indian Village Museum

The Oz Museum

Constitution Hall National Historic Landmark

Kansas Motor Speedway

Mount Sunflower

World's Largest Ball of Twine

CAWKER CITY

Republican

KANSAS CITY, MO

KANSAS CITY

Smoky Hills

MANHATTAN

Solomon

Kansas

TOPEKA ★

LAWRENCE

High Plains

Smoky Hill

SALINA

Kansas State Capitol

Strawberry Hill Museum and Cultural Center

KANSAS

GREAT BEND

Santa Fe Trail

Arkansas

Mid-America All-Indian Center

Marais des Cygnes Wildlife Area

Cimarron National Grasslands

DODGE CITY

Boot Hill and the Gunfighter Wax Museums

The Red Hills

WICHITA

Flint Hills

Verdigris

Neosho

Little House on the Prairie Museum

INDEPENDENCE

QUICK FACTS

State capital: Topeka
Largest city: Wichita
Total area: 82,277 square miles (213,096 sq km)
Highest point: Mount Sunflower, 4,039 feet (1,231 m)
Lowest point: Verdigris River, 679 feet (207 m)

0   50
Miles

OKLAHOMA

CENTRAL U.S.A.

Smith County is smack in the middle of the country—literally! (Okay, okay, only if you don't count Hawai'i and Alaska.)

WINDIEST CITY

Dodge City, a town so dangerous in the late 1800s that it was famous for its cemetery, now distinguishes itself by being America's windiest city, with average winds of 13.9 mph.

POWERFUL "BOOKS"

Beecher's Bibles aren't bibles—they're guns! The nickname was given to rifles used by antislavery factions in pre-Civil War Kansas to honor abolitionist Henry Ward Beecher.

WELL MADE WELL

Greensburg is home to the largest hand-excavated well in the world. It's 109 feet deep and 32 feet wide, and in 2008 it became one of the 8 Wonders of Kansas.

wonders
of
Kansas!
KANSAS SAMPLER FOUNDATION ©

MARIACHI (GRAND) MAMA

In 1977, Teresa Cuevas of Topeka founded Mariachi Estrella, one of the first all-female mariachi bands. As of 2008, the 88-year-old violinist was still playing with her band.

SHOESTRING BUDGET

Frugal farmer Frank Stoeber left his fellow Cawker City citizens quite a legacy when he died: the world's largest ball of sisal twine. It's currently 40 feet around, and weighs 14,587 pounds!

DRY WIT

The 19th-century explorer Zebulon Pike had his own name for the area we now call Kansas: The Great American Desert. (Okay, so it's a little dry in Kansas. So what?!)

A GOOD INVESTMENT

In 1958, two brothers borrowed $600 from their mom to open Pizza Hut in Wichita. It became an international chain, earning millions annually. Think their mom got her money back?

ON HER OWN TERMS

In 1978, Senator Nancy Kassebaum of Topeka became the first woman elected to the U.S. Senate who was not succeeding her husband. You go, girl—or rather, well done, Senator!

OLDER THAN DIRT

Hutchinson hosts what may be the world's longest living organism. An ancient salt crystal at the Kansas Underground Salt Museum contains bacteria with cells that were alive before the dinosaurs!

KANSAS

THE SUNFLOWER STATE

QUICK FACTS

State capital: Frankfort
Largest city: Louisville
Total area: 40,409 square miles
(104,659 sq km)
Highest point: Black Mountain at
4,145 feet (1,263 m)
Lowest point: At the Mississippi
River, 257 feet (78 m)

OHIO

INDIANA

ILLINOIS

MISSOURI

Mississippi

Kentucky Derby at
Churchill Downs

The Knobs

COVINGTON

Ohio

FRANKFORT

Fort Knox

Ohio River

Ohio

LOUISVILLE

Fort Boonesborough
State Park

LEXINGTON

Kentucky

OWENSBORO

KENTUCKY

Berea
College

Black
Mountain

Mammoth
Cave

BOWLING GREEN

Fisher-Ridge
Cave

Cumberland

Appalachian

Mountains

VIRGINI

Kentucky
Lake

Mississippi River

Trail of Tears
Commemorative
Park

Tallest
Tree in
Kentucky

Cumberland Gap
National
Historic Park

Appalachian
Mountains

CUMBERLAND
GAP

NORTH
CAROLIN

TENNESSEE

0   50
Miles

GOING BANANAS

The 1981 International Banana Festival in Fulton
featured a one-ton banana pudding! Was that
before or after they added the whipped cream?

HISTORY THIEVES

In 2004, four men used a Taser to steal
rare manuscripts from Transylvania
University. The theft is considered the
first armed robbery of historic docu-
ments in the U.S.

NATIVE SONS AT ODDS

President Abraham Lincoln was born
near Hodgenville, just about 100 miles
from Fairview, where Confederate
President Jefferson Davis was
born. Statues of both stand in the
Kentucky capitol building.

CHAMPION HORSE

Considered by many to be the greatest racehorse of all time, Man o' War was born in Lexington. He won 20 out of 21 races, though he never competed in the Kentucky Derby.

TONS OF GOLD

The Fort Knox Kentucky Bullion Depository is part of the Treasury Department. Its fortified vault holds about 4,603 tons of gold bullion. But don't bother dropping by; the facility is closed to visitors!

HOCKEY HIGHTAILS IT

The Lexington-based Kentucky Thoroughblades were part of the American Hockey League from 1996-2001. When Kentuckians lost interest in the cold-weather sport, the Thoroughblades split town for Cleveland, Ohio.

Stephen Foster, the "father of American music," wrote "My Old Kentucky Home," the state's official song. What's weird about this? He never even lived in Kentucky!

JUST MAKE IT UP

SIBLING STARS

Kentucky natives and sisters Loretta Lynn and Crystal Gayle both found fame as singers. Loretta, 17 years older than Crystal, often brought her little sister on tour with her.

HILLERICH HOMERUN

Bud Hillerich changed baseball forever after seeing pro Pete Browning break his bat during a game. Bud made Pete a new bat in his father's woodshop, and the Louisville Slugger was born!

MELTING-POT MINING

In 1917, the U.S. Coal & Coke Company built the world's largest coal-mining operation, Portal 31. It had 10,000 employees from 38 nations, and provided health care and education.

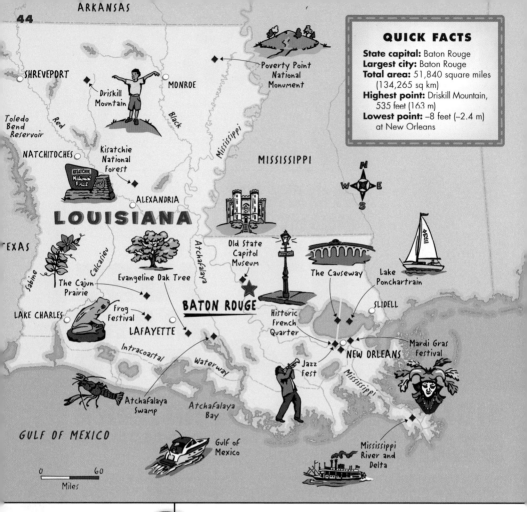

ARKANSAS

SHREVEPORT

Driskill
Mountain

MONROE

Poverty Point
National
Monument

Toledo
Bend
Reservoir

Red

Black

Mississippi

MISSISSIPPI

NATCHITOCHES

Kisatchie
National
Forest

KISATCHIE
National
Forest

LOUISIANA

ALEXANDRIA

N
W E
S

TEXAS

The Cajun
Prairie

Sabine

Calcasieu

Evangeline Oak Tree

Atchafalaya

Old State
Capitol
Museum

The Causeway

Lake
Pontchartrain

LAKE CHARLES

Frog
Festival

LAFAYETTE

BATON ROUGE

Historic
French
Quarter

SLIDELL

NEW ORLEANS

Mardi Gras
Festival

Intracoastal

Waterway

Jazz
Fest

Mississippi

Atchafalaya
Swamp

Atchafalaya
Bay

GULF OF MEXICO

Gulf of
Mexico

Mississippi
River and
Delta

0   60
Miles

QUICK FACTS

State capital: Baton Rouge
Largest city: Baton Rouge
Total area: 51,840 square miles
(134,265 sq km)
Highest point: Driskill Mountain,
535 feet (163 m)
Lowest point: –8 feet (–2.4 m)
at New Orleans

RED, HOT, & SPICY!

Edmund McIlhenny
invented Tabasco sauce
in 1868—he decided people
needed some pep in their
food as they struggled
through Reconstruction.
His family still produces it
today!

NEVER-ENDING KNOCKOUT

The longest boxing match on record lasted more than seven hours in New
Orleans in 1893. The boxers were so tired, the match had to be declared a draw.

EPIC BRIDGE

Metairie is home to the world's longest bridge over water. The Lake
Pontchartrain Causeway is 24 miles long and it reportedly takes an average
of 26 minutes to drive over it!

CAPITAL CAPITOL

At 450 feet, the Louisiana State Capitol in Baton Rouge is the tallest of the capitols in the United States. The art deco building is adorned with sculptures depicting the state's history.

PRESIDENTIAL PARDON

In 1815, Frenchman Jean Lafitte helped defeat the British at the Battle of New Orleans and later received a presidential pardon. Why did he need a pardon? He was a pirate!

CH-CH-CHING!

Louisiana produces 90% of the nation's crawfish, which has been in the area for centuries. Between commercial fishing and crawfish farming, the freshwater crustacean brings the state $120 million a year!

GET IT STRAIGHT!

Natchitoches, the oldest city in the Louisiana Purchase Territory, was founded in 1714. Don't confuse it with Nacogdoches, Texas, which is about 100 miles away—locals will get very upset!

LOTSA LAWS!

Louisiana is the only state whose legal system is a combination of common law (which the other states follow), and Spanish and French civil law. As if one legal system weren't enough!

NO SCHOOL!

In some Louisiana high schools, students get to stay home for the opening day of—wait for it—squirrel-hunting season! Maybe it's time to petition your principal . . .

EVERYONE LOVES ELLEN!

Ellen Degeneres, the comedian and talk-show host, hails from Metairie. Before hitting it big, she was a waitress, a vacuum-cleaner saleswoman, and an oyster shucker. Hilarious!

LOUISIANA

THE PELICAN STATE

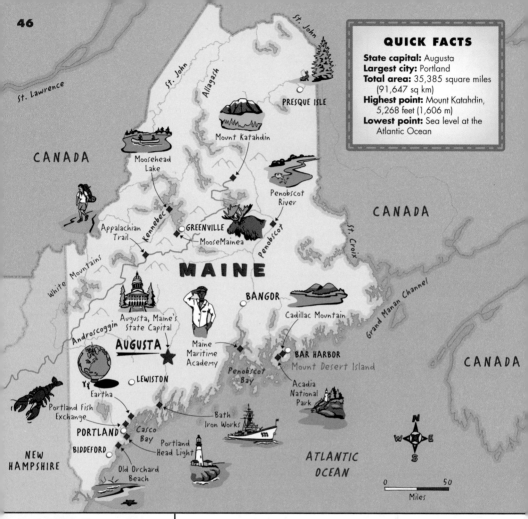

QUICK FACTS

State capital: Augusta
Largest city: Portland
Total area: 35,385 square miles (91,647 sq km)
Highest point: Mount Katahdin, 5,268 feet (1,606 m)
Lowest point: Sea level at the Atlantic Ocean

St. John

St. Lawrence

St. John

Allagash

PRESQUE ISLE

Mount Katahdin

CANADA

Moosehead Lake

Penobscot River

CANADA

Appalachian Trail

Kennebec

GREENVILLE

MooseMainea

Penobscot

St. Croix

MAINE

White Mountains

BANGOR

Cadillac Mountain

Grand Manan Channel

Androscoggin

Augusta, Maine's State Capital

AUGUSTA

Maine Maritime Academy

Penobscot Bay

BAR HARBOR
Mount Desert Island

CANADA

Eartha

○ LEWISTON

Acadia National Park

Portland Fish Exchange

Bath Iron Works

N
W   E
S

PORTLAND

Casco Bay

BIDDEFORD

Portland Head Light

ATLANTIC OCEAN

NEW HAMPSHIRE

Old Orchard Beach

0   50
Miles

HALFWAY HAMLET

The town of Perry is on the 45th parallel. So what, you say? It's the halfway point between the equator and the North Pole! (Seriously! Go look at a globe!)

WHIRLPOOL WONDER

The largest whirlpool in the western hemisphere is the Old Sow, in Eastport. (No, it's not the kind of whirlpool you sit in with your friends. It's the natural kind!)

Ever heard the expression "She's got moxie"? It comes from Maine's state beverage, Moxie, a soft drink with spunk and pep, invented by Augustin Thompson of Union in 1876.

MAINE'S MOXIE!

TOP OF THE TRAIL

Baxter State Park in northern Maine, home of Mount Katahdin, is the beginning (or the end!) of the 2,178-mile-long Appalachian Trail, the longest marked footpath in America.

AWESOME AUTHOR

North Brooklin's E. B. White wrote three children's classics that you are probably very familiar with: *Stuart Little*, *Charlotte's Web*, and *The Trumpet of the Swan*. (Don't know them? Go read one!)

In 1897, Louis Sockalexis of the Penobscot tribe of Maine became the first acknowledged Native American to play professional baseball.

A BASEBALL FIRST

HOMETOWN HORROR HERO

Portland's Stephen King is known as the master of horror. He composes many of his tales in his Bangor home, which is surrounded by a cast iron fence featuring gargoyles!

THE "LOWLY" LOBSTER

Maine is famous for its lobster—people come from far and wide to eat it. But in colonial times lobster was so abundant, it was considered food for prisoners and servants!

OLDIE BUT GOODIE

George Allen of Cherryfield patented a cool wrench in 1888 that can still be found in just about every workman's toolbox. What's it called? The Allen wrench, of course!

LAPTOPS FOR ALL!

In 2002, governor Angus King revolutionized public schools in Maine by giving every middle school student a laptop. The program has worked so well that it's still going.

MAINE

THE PINE TREE STATE

PENNSYLVANIA

Muddy Creek Falls

South Mountain Blue Ridge

Camp David

Susquehanna

Fort McHenry

NEW JERSEY

CUMBERLAND

Potomac

FREDERICK

Orioles Park at Camden Yards

WEST VIRGINIA

MARYLAND

BALTIMORE

The U.S. Naval Academy

Fort Meade

ROCKVILLE

U.S. Weather Bureau

ANNAPOLIS

Chesapeake Bay Bridge

Delaware Bay

DELAWARE

DISTRICT OF COLUMBIA

Banneker-Douglass Museum

Potomac River

SALISBURY

Assateague Island National Seashore

VIRGINIA

Patuxent

Potomac

Chesapeake Bay

Chincoteague Bay

Chesapeake Bay

N W E S

ATLANTIC OCEAN

0   30
Miles

QUICK FACTS

State capital: Annapolis
Largest city: Baltimore
Total area: 12,407 square miles (32,134 sq km)
Highest point: Hoye Crest on Backbone Mountain, 3,360 feet (1,024 m)
Lowest point: Sea level at the Atlantic Ocean

GRIDIRON POET

Famous Baltimore poet Edgar Allan Poe is held in high esteem by the National Football League! (Yes, the NFL.) The Baltimore Ravens are named after Poe's 1845 poem "The Raven."

OYSTER WARS

In the late 1800s, Maryland borrowed a cannon from the federal government to stop pirates who were after the oysters in Chesapeake Bay. (They must have been good oysters!)

BABE'S BASEBALL DESTINY

George Herman Ruth Sr., father of the legendary "Sultan of Swat," Babe Ruth, once ran Ruth's Cafe smack in the middle of what is now Oriole Park's center-field. Sounds like destiny!

WELCOME TO ORIOLE PARK CAMDEN YARDS

CRUSTACEAN QUEEN

The National Hard Crab Derby is held every Labor Day weekend in Crisfield. It has crab races and cooking contests, and even crowns a Miss Crustacean every year!

COLOR COORDINATED

Maryland's state cat, the calico, shares three colors with the state flag, the state bird (the oriole), and the state butterfly (the checkerspot): orange, black, and white.

MEDIEVAL TIMES

Maryland's official sport is jousting! Competitors ride horses and carry a lance over an 80-yard course while trying to spear suspended rings. (At least they're not trying to spear each other.)

TIME KEEPER

Mathematician and astronomer Benjamin Banneker of Ellicott Mills designed and built America's first clock in 1753. It was made entirely out of wood and ran perfectly for over 30 years!

FISHERMAN LINGO

Maryland fishermen may sound like they're speaking a foreign language when they talk about jimmies, sooks, and busters, but they're really just talking about crabs!

LADY DAY

Billie Holiday, one of the world's greatest jazz singers, grew up in Baltimore. A statue of "Lady Day," as she was known, stands in Druid Hill.

CIVIL WAR SURVIVOR

The USS *Constellation*, docked in Baltimore's Inner Harbor, is the last surviving ship from the Civil War. The ship served America for 100 years and is now a museum.

MAINE

VERMONT

NEW HAMPSHIRE

ATLANTIC OCEAN

NEW YORK

Natural Bridge State Park

The Big Chair

Walden Pond

LOWELL

GLOUCESTER

NORTH ADAMS

Berkshire Taconic Region

Concord and Lexington

SALEM

Old North Church, Boston

Mount Greylock

PITTSFIELD

LEOMINSTER

LEXINGTON

MASSACHUSETTS

WORCESTER

Harvard University

BOSTON

Charles

Boston Common

Provincetown

SPRINGFIELD

Naismith Memorial Basketball Hall of Fame

RHODE ISLAND

PLYMOUTH

CAPE COD BAY

CONNECTICUT

NEW BEDFORD

HYANNIS

Cape Cod

Aquinnah Cliffs

New Bedford Whaling National Historic Park

Nantucket Island

Martha's Vineyard

ATLANTIC OCEAN

Connecticut Valley

Connecticut

QUICK FACTS

State capital: Boston
Largest city: Boston
Total area: 10,555 square miles (27,337 sq km)
Highest point: Mount Greylock at 3,491 feet (1,064 m) above sea level
Lowest point: Sea level along the Atlantic Ocean

0   20
Miles

TALENTED TRICKSTERS

The Massachusetts Institute of Technology is famous for cranking out geniuses—and for the crazy pranks its geniuses pull off, like putting a fire truck on the dome of a building.

WRITING ON THE WALL

In 1922 in Rockport, Swedish immigrant Ellis Stenman built a two-room house—and all its furnishings—out of over 100,000 newspapers. Bet he never ran out of things to read.

TRANSLATION, PLEASE?

Lake Chargoggagoggmanchauggagoggchaubunagungamaugg, in Webster, has the longest name in American geography. According to some sources, it means, "You fish on your side, I fish on my side, and no one fishes in the middle."

CONSISTENT COOKING

In 1896, Fannie Farmer of Medford published the first cookbook to use standard measurements such as the teaspoon and tablespoon—and it's still in print over 100 years later!

SAM I AM

In 1812, Arlington's Samuel Wilson supplied the army with meat in containers stamped "U.S." Soldiers joked that "U.S." stood for Uncle Sam, and a great American symbol was born!

BABY SPOCK

Are you a *Star Trek* fan? Make a pilgrimage to Boston, where Leonard Nimoy—known to Trekkies as the half-Vulcan, half-human Spock—was born. Just watch out for the Vulcan nerve pinch!

Raytheon, a technology company in Waltham, created the first microwave in 1947. It was called a Radarange, it was as big as a refrigerator, and it cost between $2,000 and $3,000.

MICROWAVE MAGIC

DELICIOUS DISCOVERY

In 1930, Ruth Wakefield broke a chocolate bar into pieces for her cookie batter at the Toll House Inn in Whitman. The pieces didn't melt, and chocolate chips were born!

MOLASSES DISASTER

In 1919, a wave of molasses estimated at between 8 and 40 feet high flooded Boston's North End at 35 miles per hour after a tank containing 2.3 million gallons of the sticky stuff collapsed.

Clinton is home to the nation's oldest baseball diamond, which opened for play in 1878 and has hosted regular games of the great American pastime ever since!

FIRST FIELD

Copper Harbor

LAKE SUPERIOR

CANADA

HOUGHTON

Keweenaw Peninsula

Marquette Harbor Lighthouse

Great Lakes Shipwreck Museum

Sault Ste. Marie

MARQUETTE

Upper Peninsula   SAULT STE. MARIE

MICHIGAN

Porcupine Mountains

Menominee

National Ski Hall of Fame

Straits of Mackinac

Mackinac Island

LAKE MICHIGAN

LAKE HURON

Sleeping Bear Dunes National Lakeshore

N W E S

0   30
Miles

WISCONSIN

TRAVERSE CITY

Manistee

Au Sable

Sanilac Petroglyphs

National Cherry Festival

CADILLAC

Lower Peninsula

Muskegon

Saginaw Children's Zoo

Cass

SAGINAW

Shiawassee

CANADA

QUICK FACTS

State capital: Lansing
Largest city: Detroit
Total area: 96,716 square miles
(250,494 sq km)
Highest point: Mount Arvon,
1,979 feet (603 m)
Lowest point: 571 feet (174 m)
along Lake Erie

GRAND RAPIDS

HOLLAND

LANSING

Grand

Spirit of Detroit

DETROIT

Holland Tulip Festival

ANN ARBOR

Henry Ford Museum and Greenfield Village

Motown

LAKE ERIE

St. Joseph

INDIANA

OHIO

MICHIGAN LOVES MADONNA

Madonna is a Michigan girl! The Queen of Pop was born in Bay City, and grew up in Rochester Hills. She left when she was 20, to pursue dancing in New York.

BRIDGE STATS

At 8,614 feet, the Mackinac Bridge is the longest suspension bridge in the western hemisphere. The bridge's deck is designed to move as much as 35 feet in high winds!

PENINSULA PARTY

Michigan's motto is, "If you seek a pleasant peninsula, look about you." Why? It's the only state with two peninsulas. (The Lower Peninsula looks like a giant mitten!)

SERIOUS ABOUT CEREAL

Important decisions about your breakfast cereal were probably made in Battle Creek, where, at one time, both Kellogg's and Post were headquartered. The companies were archrivals for years!

CREATIVE CAPITOL

The Michigan State Capitol building has more than nine acres of hand-painted surfaces! Designs include animals, flowers, trees, and even a mythical beast called a winged griffin.

ELVIS FEST!

The Michigan Elvis Fest in Ypsilanti is one of the largest tribute concerts in North America. The country's best Elvis impersonators honor the King in July, on the anniversary of his death.

LAKES APLENTY

Michigan has 11,000 lakes and 36,000 miles of streams. You can find water within 6 miles of wherever you are in the state! (Don't visit if you suffer from aquaphobia.)

SKIING HISTORY

We have Scandinavian immigrant miners and lumberjacks to thank for introducing skiing as a sport to the Ishpeming area, which is now home to the U.S. National Ski and Snowboard Hall of Fame.

MOTOWN MAN

Berry Gordy founded Motown Records in Detroit in 1959. It was the first music label owned by an African American to feature black artists who were popular across racial lines.

TREMENDOUS TIRE

Detroit has the world's largest tire, which started life as a Ferris wheel at the New York World's Fair in 1964. The 80-foot-tall, 12-ton tire has treads big enough to fit your head!

MICHIGAN

THE GREAT LAKES STATE

CANADA

Red River Valley

Lake of the Woods

Rainy Lake

Rainy

INTERNATIONAL FALLS

Boundary Waters Canoe Area Wilderness

Grand Portage National Monument

Upper Red Lake

Lower Red Lake

Ironworld Discovery Center

Superior Upland

LAKE SUPERIOR

NORTH DAKOTA

Red

Paul Bunyan and Babe the Blue Ox

BEMIDJI

Lake Itasca

MOORHEAD

GRAND RAPIDS

Forest History Center

DULUTH

MICHIGAN

MINNESOTA

BRAINERD

Mille Lacs Lake

Lake Superior Marine Museum Association

Runestone Museum

St. Croix

ST. CLOUD

Mississippi

Hubert H. Humphrey Metrodome

WISCONSIN

SOUTH DAKOTA

Minneapolis Institute of Arts

ST. PAUL

MINNEAPOLIS

Minnesota

AMERICA

Mall of America

Historic Fort Snelling

Science Museum of Minnesota

Pipestone National Monument

MANKATO

Jolly Green Giant Statue

ROCHESTER

Transparent Man

Mississippi

IOWA

QUICK FACTS

State capital: Saint Paul
Largest city: Minneapolis
Total area: 86,939 square miles (225,171 sq km)
Highest point: Eagle Mountain at 2,301 feet (701 m)
Lowest point: Lake Superior at 601 feet (183 m)

N
W E
S

0   50
Miles

HOCKEY MANIA

Eveleth, home to the Hockey Hall of Fame, is known as the Capital of American Hockey because the city has contributed more professional players per capita than any other.

BRRRRRR!!!!

Embarrass is known as the nation's "Cold Spot." On February 2, 1996, Embarrass experienced one of lowest temperatures ever recorded in the Lower 48: -57°F!

MISSISSIPPI IN MINNESOTA

Lake Itasca, in Minnesota's Lake Itasca State Park, is the source—or starting point—for the mighty Mississippi River, once the country's most important transportation route.

ICE PALACE

The Saint Paul Winter Carnival, which is the oldest and largest winter festival in the nation, is reported to have featured an ice palace made of over 30,000 blocks of ice!

SUPER SHORES

Minnesota, "land of 10,000 lakes," has 90,000 miles of shoreline. That's more than California, Florida, and Hawai'i combined! (No wonder there's one boat for every six people in the state.)

MALL MANIA!

The Mall of America in Bloomington is the world's largest indoor shopping mall. An average of 11,000 people work in the mall, which is the size of 78 football fields!

BIG BUNYAN

Akeley may be small—the population hovers around 400—but it has a huge, 25-foot statue of Paul Bunyan. Go visit and sit in the mythological lumberjack's palm!

VIKING GRAFFITI

Some think that a runestone—an ancient stone with an inscription—found on a Douglas County farm, now in a museum in Alexandria, proves that the Vikings explored North America nearly 130 years before Christopher Columbus.

OVER THE RAINBOW

Grand Rapids is the birthplace of *The Wizard of Oz* star Judy Garland. If there's "no place like home," there must be no place like Grand Rapids!

HOT AIR

The Metrodome in Minneapolis is inflatable! It requires 250,000 cubic feet of air pressure per minute, and visitors use revolving doors to keep air from escaping.

MINNESOTA—THE NORTH STAR STATE

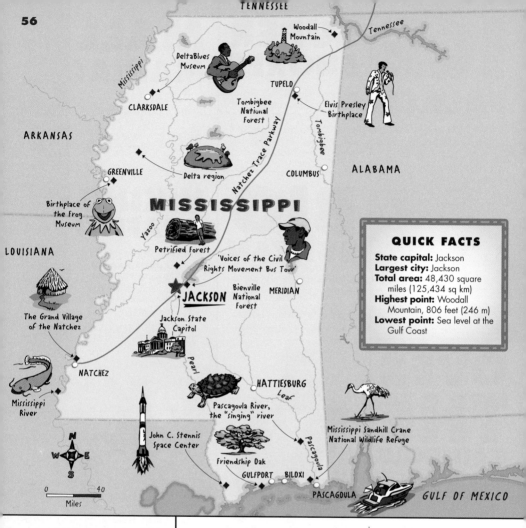

TENNESSEE

Woodall Mountain

Tennessee

Mississippi

DeltaBlues Museum

CLARKSDALE

Tombigbee National Forest

TUPELO

Elvis Presley Birthplace

ARKANSAS

GREENVILLE

Delta region

Tombigbee

ALABAMA

COLUMBUS

Natchez Trace Parkway

MISSISSIPPI

Birthplace of the Frog Museum

LOUISIANA

Yazoo

Petrified forest

'Voices of the Civil Rights Movement Bus Tour'

JACKSON

Bienville National Forest

MERIDIAN

Jackson State Capitol

The Grand Village of the Natchez

NATCHEZ

Pearl

Mississippi River

HATTIESBURG

Leaf

Pascagoula River, the "singing" river

Mississippi Sandhill Crane National Wildlife Refuge

Pascagoula

John C. Stennis Space Center

Friendship Oak

GULFPORT

BILOXI

PASCAGOULA

GULF OF MEXICO

N W E S
0   40
Miles

QUICK FACTS

State capital: Jackson
Largest city: Jackson
Total area: 48,430 square miles (125,434 sq km)
Highest point: Woodall Mountain, 806 feet (246 m)
Lowest point: Sea level at the Gulf Coast

FLYING TURTLE

In the late 1880s, a gopher turtle completely encased in ice fell to the ground in Bovina during a May hailstorm. (Huh? Yeah. No one has any idea how this happened.)

LITERARY LEGEND

Eudora Welty of Jackson won every major prize for writing—except the Nobel Prize for Literature. She was originally a photographer, but literature won her heart and she never looked back.

FLOODED FOREST

The "Grand Canyon of Mississippi" is a 36-million-year-old petrified forest in Flora. The 100-foot-tall trees were swept away by a flood. (That must have been some flood!)

BIRTH OF B.B.

On September 16, 1925, Riley B. King was born in Itta Bena. In 1949, he changed his name to B.B. King—B.B. for "Blues Boy"—and quickly became a blues legend.

CITIZEN REBEL

Mississippi resident Jefferson Davis had his citizenship revoked in 1861, when he became the Confederate President. It was restored by President Jimmy Carter in 1978, 89 years after Davis died.

SHOE REVOLUTION

In 1884, Phil Gilbert's Shoe Parlor in Vicksburg made history when it started selling pairs of shoes in boxes. Prior to that, shoes were sold individually. (Weird, right?!)

FIT FOR A KING

In 1935, Elvis Presley was born in Tupelo. The "shotgun shack" where he was born is part of the Elvis Presley Museum, which brings in $46 million a year!

29 USA
ROCK & ROLL SINGER, 1935–1977
ELVIS PRESLEY

TOY HISTORY

President Theodore Roosevelt was hunting near Onward when he refused to shoot a helpless bear. A toy merchant then honored the kind president with a stuffed animal named "Teddy's Bear."

WHAT'S IN A NAME?

Mississippi is named for the mighty river that flows through it. The name comes from the Chippewa Indian words *mici zipi*, which mean "great river."

CREATION OF KERMIT

Jim Henson grew up playing on the banks of Deer Creek in Leland. Deer Creek is said to be the birthplace of his first Muppet invention, Kermit the Frog.

MISSISSIPPI THE MAGNOLIA STATE

58

QUICK FACTS

State capital: Jefferson City
Largest city: Kansas City
Total area: 69,704 square miles (180,533 sq km)
Highest point: Taum Sauk Mountain, 1,772 feet (540 m), in Iron County
Lowest point: St. Francis River, 230 feet (70 m), in Dunklin County

IOWA

NEB.

ST. JOSEPH
Negro Leagues Baseball Museum

KANSAS CITY
American Jazz Museum

Toy and Miniature Museum

Mark Twain Birthplace and State Historic Site

HANNIBAL

Mississippi

Mark Twain Lake
Graham Cave State Park

COLUMBIA

Missouri State Capitol

JEFFERSON CITY ★

MISSOURI

The City Museum

Gateway Arch

ST. CHARLES

ST. LOUIS

International Bowling Museum Hall of Fame

Missouri

KANSAS

Harry S Truman Birthplace

Osage

Lake of the Ozarks

Missouri State Museum

Missouri Sports Hall of Fame

SPRINGFIELD

JOPLIN

George Washington Carver National Monument

Ozark Plateau

Trail of Tears State Park

ILLINOIS

CAPE GIRARDEAU

Laura Ingalls Wilder Historic Home and Museum

St. Francis

Mississippi Alluvial Plain

KENT

TENNESSEE

OKLAHOMA

N W E S

0   40
Miles

ARKANSAS

STEAMBOAT GRAVE

In 1856, the steamboat *Arabia* sank in the Missouri River. In 1988, excavators found it in a cornfield, a half mile away from the river and 45 feet underground!

DELICIOUS DEBUT!

Ice cream cones and iced tea had their debut at the St. Louis World's Fair in 1904. Let's all take a moment now to say a proper thank you!

MISSOURI MONIKER

Hannibal steamboat pilot Samuel Clemens—aka Mark Twain—took his pen name from the boatman's cry, "By the mark twain!" which alerted pilots to shallow water on the Mississippi.

George Washington Carver

32 USA

AWESOME ARCH

At 630 feet, the Jefferson National Memorial, also known as the Gateway Arch, is twice the height of the Statue of Liberty. It's America's tallest national monument!

MAIN STREET MODEL

Walt Disney lived in Marceline as a boy and loved the quintessential small town so much that he used it as the model for Disneyland's Main Street, USA.

PEANUT MAGIC

Chemist George Washington Carver, born near Diamond, revitalized the South's economy and changed agricultural practices and diet with his discovery that growing peanuts could improve soil quality.

FOUNTAIN CITY

Kansas City has more fountains than any other city in the world, except Rome, Italy. The first fountains were originally built to provide clean drinking water for animals.

MAN-MADE PARADISE

Bonne Terre is home to a former lead mine that was flooded with billions of gallons of water and turned into the world's largest underground resort for diving.

GREATEST THING SINCE . . .

The Chillicothe Baking Company sold the first loaf of sliced bread in 1928, thanks to the newly invented bread slicer. In 2007, Chillicothe officially became the "Home of Sliced Bread."

In 1811, New Madrid experienced an earthquake of such severity that parts of the Mississippi River actually flowed backward!

CRAZY CURRENT

MISSOURI

THE SHOW ME STATE

CANADA

Kootenai National Forest

Glacier National Park

Milk

Louis Toavs John Deere Tractor Collection and Museum

KALISPELL

Lewis and Clark National Historic Trail Interpretive Center

Montana Historical Society

Rocky

Flathead Lake

Clark

Missouri

GREAT FALLS

Fort Peck Lake

NORTH DAKOTA

National Bison Range

MISSOULA

Fork

HELENA

MONTANA

Western Heritage Center

Musselshell

Yellowstone

MILES CITY

Elkhorn Ghost Town

BUTTE

Mountains

Granite Peak

BILLINGS

Custer National Forest

The World Museum of Mining

BOZEMAN

Bighorn

IDAHO

Yellowstone National Park Gateways

Little Bighorn Battlefield National Monument

SOUTH DAKOTA

QUICK FACTS

State capital: Helena
Largest city: Billings
Total area: 147,042 square miles (380,837 sq km)
Highest point: Granite Peak, 12,799 feet (3,901 m), in Park County
Lowest point: Kootenai River in Lincoln County, 1,800 feet (549 m)

WYOMING

NEBRA

N
W   E
S

0   50
Miles

BONE
BREAKTHROUGH

In 1978, a rock shop owner found a group of baby dinosaur bones near Choteau. The site, now called Egg Mountain, is rich in fossilized dinosaur eggs and baby skeletons.

WOMAN FOR PEACE

In 1917, Missoula's Jeanette Rankin became the first woman to serve in Congress. She also holds the distinction of being the only representative to vote against U.S. involvement in World War II.

WORLD RECORD

Thanks to elementary school kids in Great Falls, the 201-foot-long Roe River was listed in the *Guinness Book of World Records* as the shortest river in the world!

FROM FREEZING TO FINE

Loma holds the record for the greatest temperature change in a single day. On January 14-15, 1972, the temperature went from -59°F to 49°F!

DRAGON DRAMA

Christopher Paolini, the teenage author of *Eragon*, grew up in Paradise Valley. The natural beauty surrounding him—including mountains called the Crazies—inspired the dramatic settings in his books.

SIGN HERE!

When William Clark carved his signature and the date—July 25, 1806—into a rock at Pompeys Pillar, he left the only known physical evidence of Lewis and Clark's expedition.

GOLD RUSH MILLIONAIRES

In 1888, Helena had more millionaires per capita than any other city in the world. About $3.6 billion worth of the sparkly stuff was mined in the area during the gold rush.

WHERE GUSH THE **GEYSERS**

OREGON SHORT LINE
ALL RAIL ROUTE TO THE
YELLOWSTONE

According to the NPS, Yellowstone Park has 300 geysers. No, not geezers—geysers! Geysers are hot springs that erupt. The park, also known as Geyserland, is home to two-thirds of the world's spouting springs.

GREAT GEYSERLAND

GRAND SLAM!

The only pitcher ever to hit a grand slam in the World Series is Dave McNally from Billings. The Baltimore Oriole made history in 1970, against the Cincinnati Reds.

RUN, DOGS, RUN!

The Race to the Sky covers hundreds of miles. Mushers follow trails through wilderness areas and climb to an altitude of 6,000 feet. The race starts with a vet check, to make sure the dogs are ready to dash.

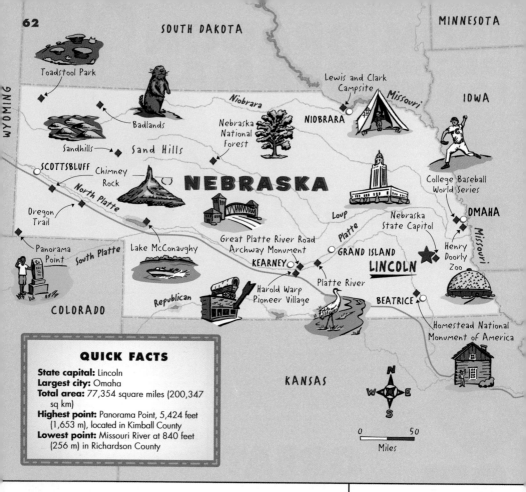

SOUTH DAKOTA

MINNESOTA

WYOMING

Toadstool Park

Badlands

Sandhills — Sand Hills

Niobrara

Lewis and Clark Campsite

Missouri

IOWA

NIOBRARA

Nebraska National Forest

SCOTTSBLUFF Chimney Rock

North Platte

NEBRASKA

Nebraska State Capitol

College Baseball World Series

OMAHA

Oregon Trail

Panorama Point South Platte

Lake McConaughy

Great Platte River Road Archway Monument

KEARNEY

Loup

Platte

GRAND ISLAND

LINCOLN

Henry Doorly Zoo

Missouri

Republican

Harold Warp Pioneer Village

Platte River

BEATRICE

COLORADO

Homestead National Monument of America

QUICK FACTS

State capital: Lincoln
Largest city: Omaha
Total area: 77,354 square miles (200,347 sq km)
Highest point: Panorama Point, 5,424 feet (1,653 m), located in Kimball County
Lowest point: Missouri River at 840 feet (256 m) in Richardson County

KANSAS

N
W   E
S

0   50
Miles

CRANE-I-NESS!

From February to April, thousands of tourists travel to the Platte River to watch a half million Sandhill cranes nest, feed, and store up energy for their migration.

CAR ART

Heard of Stonehenge, that cool arrangement of ancient stone slabs in England? Well, how about Carhenge? Alliance has an homage to Stonehenge made out of upended cars.

DIFFERENT STROKES

Nebraska is the only state with a unicameral legislature, meaning that it has only one house of government, the senate. All other states have both the house and the senate.

POWERFUL RESISTANCE

Red Cloud, a Lakota Indian born near North Platte in 1822, devoted his life to resisting conquest by the U.S. government, using both peaceful and violent methods.

FATHER OF THE RODEO

The performer Buffalo Bill Cody started his "Buffalo Bill's Wild West" show in North Platte in 1883, hiring real cowboys and cowgirls to demonstrate bronco riding and roping.

THE LIBERTY SWING

Hebron's claim to fame is a giant "porch" swing made for the town's 4th of July celebration that can hold up to 16 adults—or 32 kids—at one time.

ALL HAIL!

On June 22, 2003, a giant-sized hailstone fell in Aurora during a thunderstorm. Thanks to quick-thinking locals, the record-breaking ice ball was preserved—in a freezer, of course.

"HEY, KIDS!"

Edwin Perkins of Hastings invented Kool-Ade (now Kool-Aid)—earlier called Fruit Smack—in 1927. By 1950, his company was producing nearly a million packets of Kool-Aid a day!

SMALL HALL

Maskell is home to the nation's smallest city hall. How small is "smallest," you ask? Pretty small! About 10 feet by 10 feet. (Hopefully Maskell's mayor is small, too.)

YAKITY YAK

Nebraska has one of North America's greatest herds of yak, a big, wooly creature that looks like a bull and is normally found in the Himalayas in Asia.

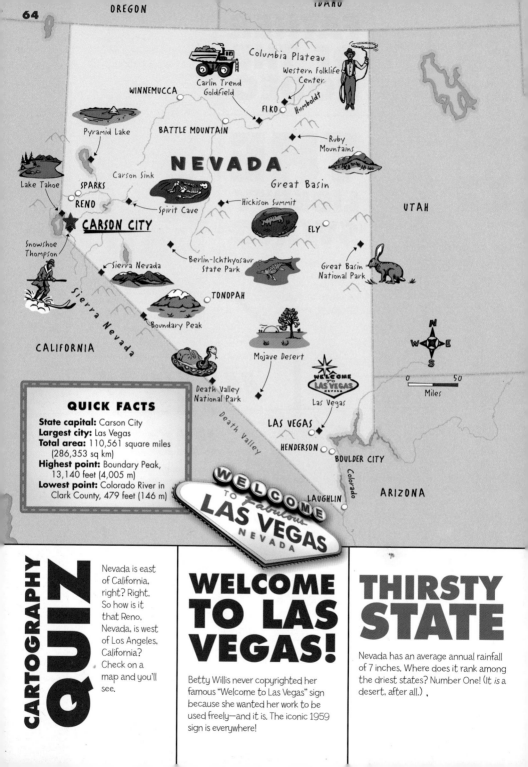

OREGON

IDAHO

Columbia Plateau

Carlin Trend Goldfield

Western Folklife Center

WINNEMUCCA

ELKO

Humboldt

Pyramid Lake

BATTLE MOUNTAIN

Ruby Mountains

NEVADA

Carson Sink

Great Basin

SPARKS

Lake Tahoe

RENO

Spirit Cave

Hickison Summit

ELY

UTAH

Snowshoe Thompson

CARSON CITY

Sierra Nevada

Berlin-Ichthyosaur State Park

Great Basin National Park

TONOPAH

Boundary Peak

Sierra Nevada

CALIFORNIA

Mojave Desert

Death Valley National Park

Las Vegas

N W E S

0   50
Miles

Death Valley

LAS VEGAS

HENDERSON

BOULDER CITY

Colorado

LAUGHLIN

ARIZONA

QUICK FACTS

State capital: Carson City
Largest city: Las Vegas
Total area: 110,561 square miles (286,353 sq km)
Highest point: Boundary Peak, 13,140 feet (4,005 m)
Lowest point: Colorado River in Clark County, 479 feet (146 m)

WELCOME TO Fabulous **LAS VEGAS** NEVADA

CARTOGRAPHY QUIZ

Nevada is east of California, right? Right. So how is it that Reno, Nevada, is west of Los Angeles, California? Check on a map and you'll see.

WELCOME TO LAS VEGAS!

Betty Willis never copyrighted her famous "Welcome to Las Vegas" sign because she wanted her work to be used freely—and it is. The iconic 1959 sign is everywhere!

THIRSTY STATE

Nevada has an average annual rainfall of 7 inches. Where does it rank among the driest states? Number One! (It *is* a desert, after all.)

DESERTED DESERT TOWN

The population of Survival Town is. . . zero! The federal government built the city—complete with houses and offices—in the desert to test the effects of a nuclear explosion in 1955.

Lake Tahoe, in the Sierra Nevada mountains, is the largest, highest alpine lake in North America. It's pretty old, too—it was formed about 2 million years ago!

WAY UP THERE

GOLDEN STATE

Elko hosts the nation's biggest open-pit gold mine, called Goldstrike. Nevada produces more gold than any other state. No wonder people go there to strike it rich!

READY, SET . . . CAMEL!

Virginia City hosts the International Camel Races every year, despite the fact that the race originated as a joke in a newspaper in 1959.

BURNING MAN

Every year, thousands journey to the Black Rock Desert to participate in an intense, week-long art festival called Burning Man, which culminates in the burning of a giant "man" sculpture.

Las Vegas's favorite son, Andre Agassi, was one of the world's greatest tennis players before he retired in 2006. He won eight grand slams and an Olympic medal.

ANDRE THE GREAT

COSTLY COMMUNIQUÉ!

In order to meet the deadline for statehood in 1864, Nevada sent its entire constitution to Washington, D.C., by telegraph. The telegraph cost $3,400—that's nearly $47,000 by today's standards!

CANADA

Space Needle
SEATTLE
WASHINGTON
OLYMPIA ★
Mount Rainier
National Park

SALEM ★
Mount Hood
OREGON
Wild Horses
of Oregon
Crater Lake
National Park

PACIFIC OCEAN

Glacier
National Park
HELENA
MONTANA
Little Bighorn Battlefield
National Monument

National State
Bison Range

Geographical Ce
North Amer
NORTH DAKO
★ BISMARCK
World's Largest Bison

Corn Palace

SOUTH DAKO
★ PIERRE

Mount Rushmore
National Memorial

Craters of the Moon
National Monument
BOISE ★
IDAHO
Lewis and Clark
National Historic Trail

Yellowstone
National Park

WYOMING

Independence
Rock
CHEYENNE ★

Chimney Rock National
Historic Site

NEBRASKA

Prairie Dog Towns

Lassen Volcanic
National Park
Fisherman's
Wharf
SACRAMENTO ★
SAN FRANCISCO

Ruby Mountains
Lake Tahoe
NEVADA
★ CARSON CITY

Marshall Gold
Discovery State
Historic Park

GREAT
SALT
LAKE
SALT LAKE CITY ●
Dinosaur
National
Monument
UTAH
Rainbow Bridge
National Monument

Pikes Peak in the
Rocky Mountains
DENVER ●
COLORADO
Colorado River

Tallgrass
Prairie
KAN

CALIFORNIA

WELCOME
LAS VEGAS
Las Vegas
LAS VEGAS

Joshua Tree
National Park
Hollywood
OSCAR
LOS ANGELES

Sea World

Grand Canyon
National Park
ARIZONA
PHOENIX ★
Sonoran
Desert

Four Corners
Monument
SANTA FE ★
NEW MEXICO
Taos Pueblo

Carlsbad Caverns

Longhorn
Ranching

OK
OKLAHOMA

Odessa Meteor Crater

We
C

The Alamo
TEXAS

Au

ALASKA (inset)
Trans-Alaska
Pipeline
ALASKA
CANADA
Mount McKinley
(Denali)
ANCHORAGE ●
JUNEAU ●
PACIFIC
OCEAN

MEXICO

Rio Grande

Lyndo
Spac

HAWAI'I (inset)
PACIFIC OCEAN
HONOLULU ★
HAWAI'I
Hawai'i Volcanoes
National Park

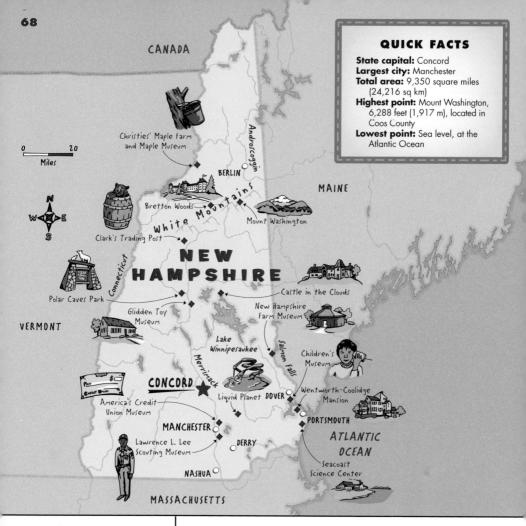

CANADA

MAINE

VERMONT

CANADA

QUICK FACTS

State capital: Concord
Largest city: Manchester
Total area: 9,350 square miles
(24,216 sq km)
Highest point: Mount Washington,
6,288 feet (1,917 m), located in
Coos County
Lowest point: Sea level, at the
Atlantic Ocean

Christies' Maple Farm
and Maple Museum

Androscoggin

BERLIN

0   20
Miles

N
W   E
S

Bretton Woods

Mount Washington

White Mountains

Clark's Trading Post

NEW HAMPSHIRE

Connecticut

Polar Caves Park

Castle in the Clouds

Glidden Toy
Museum

New Hampshire
Farm Museum

VERMONT

Lake
Winnipesaukee

Salmon Falls

Children's
Museum

Merrimack

CONCORD

Liquid Planet

DOVER

Wentworth-Coolidge
Mansion

America's Credit
Union Museum

PORTSMOUTH

MANCHESTER

ATLANTIC
OCEAN

Lawrence L. Lee
Scouting Museum

DERRY

NASHUA

Seacoast
Science Center

MASSACHUSETTS

BRILLIANT BEARS

Want to see a bear eat
ice cream? Visit Clark's
Trading Post in
Lincoln, where daily
bear shows involve
"bearsketball,"
balancing acts,
and drinking
out of "bear
cans."

ANCIENT ARTS

Want to learn how to be a blacksmith or a cooper? Apply to New Hampshire's
Traditional Arts apprentice program and keep the old arts alive by learning from
a master.

REPUBLICAN REBELS

In 1853, in Exeter, Amos Tuck called a
secret meeting of politicians who were
opposed to the Democrats, suggest-
ing they form their own party, the
Republicans. And so it began!

TRAVELING IN STYLE

In 1938, the first tramway was built, carrying people to the top of Cannon Mountain in Franconia Notch. Nearly 7 million people rode it before it was replaced in 1980.

RISE AND SHINE

Levi Hutchins of Concord was the first American to be woken up by an alarm clock, which he invented in 1787. School kids everywhere can thank Levi (or not).

TALL AND BLUSTERY

Mount Washington is the highest peak in the northeast. It is 6,288 feet and holds the record for the highest wind gust recorded on the earth's surface: 231 mph!

General John Stark of Londonderry penned New Hampshire's motto, "Live free or die." But that's only half of what he wrote. The rest is, "Death is not the worst of evils."

EXTREME MOTTO

PLACE OF PEACE

President Theodore Roosevelt won a Nobel Peace Prize for bringing Russia and Japan together in Portsmouth to sign the Treaty of Portsmouth in 1905, which ended the Russo-Japanese war.

PLASTICS GENIUS

Earl Tupper of Berlin invented an extremely popular food storage system and started his company in 1938. Can you guess what he invented? (Hint: check out his last name!) Yup—Tupperware!

COTTON GIANT

The Amoskeag Manufacturing Company in Manchester was the largest cotton textile mill in the world in the early 20th century. The mill made cloth for just about everything—even Levi's jeans!

NEW HAMPSHIRE
THE GRANITE STATE

NEW YORK

CONNECTICUT

Hudson

Delaware

Kittatinny Mountains

Great Valley

Lambert Castle

Delaware Water Gap

PATERSON

Passaic Falls

George Washington Bridge

PASSAIC

PHILLIPSBURG

Great Swamp

NEWARK

Raritan

NEW YORK

Liberty State Park

PENNSYLVANIA

ELIZABETH

PERTH AMBOY

Sandy Hook Lighthouse

ATLANTIC OCEAN

New Jersey Turnpike

Princeton University

PRINCETON

LONG BRANCH

★ TRENTON

N W E S

NEW JERSEY

New Jersey Shore

0 20
Miles

Hadrosaurus Sculpture

CAMDEN

The Pinelands

Pine Barrens

Barrier Islands

VINELAND

Lucy the Elephant

Atlantic City Boardwalk

ATLANTIC CITY

MARGATE CITY

MARYLAND

DELAWARE

Delaware Bay

Cape May

Cape May

QUICK FACTS

State capital: Trenton
Largest city: Newark
Total area: 8,721 square miles (22,588 sq km)
Highest point: High Point, 1,803 feet (550 m) above sea level
Lowest point: Sea level along Atlantic Ocean

When Thomas Edison invented the phonograph in 1877 in Menlo Park, he tested it by recording—and playing back—"Mary Had a Little Lamb."

TESTING, TESTING

EDISON GOLD MOULD RECORD

FORCEFUL PHOTOS

Dorothea Lange, one of the country's most important photographers, was born in Hoboken. Lange is famous for her striking Depression-era photos of farmers and migrant workers.

HIGHEST LAND

The appropriately named Highlands has the—wait for it—highest elevation of any coastal city from Texas to Maine. It's 226 feet above sea level. You should see the view!

SUBMARINE SUCCESS

John Holland built the first successful submarine in 1900 in Elizabethport. He sold it to the Navy for $150,000 and they named it the USS *Holland*, in his honor.

DINER DENSITY

New Jersey has one of the highest population densities in the country: about 1,175 people per square mile. Maybe that's why the state also has the most diners in the world!

EPIC POEM

William Carlos Williams, a great American poet and a doctor from Rutherford, wrote an epic poem called *Paterson*, about the industrial city. It was originally over five books long!

A TELLING TITLE

The New Jersey seaport Elizabeth calls itself "America's Containership Capital." With a reported 23 cranes, 1 million square feet of storage space, and its own on-dock railroad system, it's earned that title!

DEMANDING THE VOTE

Suffragette Alice Paul of Mount Laurel was jailed for demonstrating at the White House in 1917. Prison doctors tried to have her declared insane in order to discredit her.

E PAUL
EVEN MONTHS
BECAUSE
SED A POLITICAL PARTY
DEMAND
BE TREATED AS A
ical OFFENDER

THE SUFFRAGE PRISONERS
WERE ARRESTED FOR A
POLITICAL OFFENSE.
WE DEMAND
THAT THEY BE TREATED AS
POLITICAL OFFENDERS.

TO ASK FREEDOM
FOR WOMEN IS NOT
A CRIME
SUFFRAGE PRISONER
SHOULD NOT BE TREATED
AS CRIMINALS

HUT, HUT, HIKE!

The first college football game was played in New Brunswick between the College of New Jersey (now known as Princeton) and Rutgers College (now known as Rutgers University) in 1869.

SECRETS OF THE GAME

Charles Darrow, the inventor of Monopoly, spent his summers in Atlantic City. He loved the city so much, he borrowed its street names for his game!

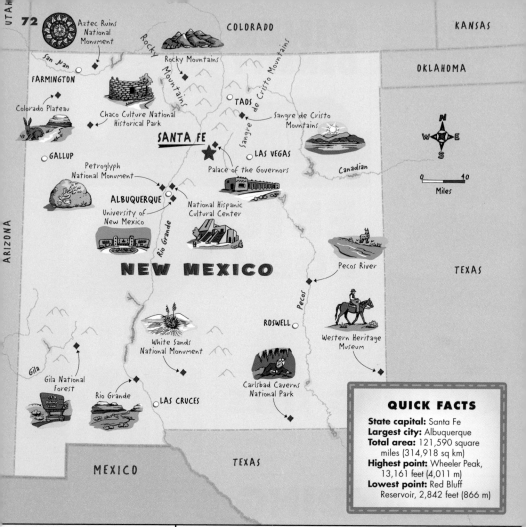

UTAH

Aztec Ruins National Monument

San Juan

FARMINGTON

Colorado Plateau

Rocky Mountains

COLORADO

KANSAS

OKLAHOMA

Rocky Mountains

Chaco Culture National Historical Park

GALLUP

SANTA FE

TAOS

Sangre de Cristo Mountains

Sangre de Cristo Mountains

LAS VEGAS

Palace of the Governors

Canadian

Petroglyph National Monument

ALBUQUERQUE

University of New Mexico

National Hispanic Cultural Center

Rio Grande

NEW MEXICO

Pecos River

TEXAS

ARIZONA

Pecos

White Sands National Monument

ROSWELL

Western Heritage Museum

Gila

Gila National Forest

Rio Grande

LAS CRUCES

Carlsbad Caverns National Park

MEXICO

TEXAS

N
W E
S

0 — 40
Miles

QUICK FACTS

State capital: Santa Fe
Largest city: Albuquerque
Total area: 121,590 square miles (314,918 sq km)
Highest point: Wheeler Peak, 13,161 feet (4,011 m)
Lowest point: Red Bluff Reservoir, 2,842 feet (866 m)

POLITICAL PARADE

In 1871, Democrats and Republicans paraded through Mesilla, and things got violent. The ensuing fight became known as the "Battle of the Bands," because both parties had marching bands!

INSPIRATION IN ALBUQUERQUE

In 1975, Bill Gates took a leave of absence from Harvard to work at a company in Albuquerque that had just built the first microcomputer. A year later, he trade-marked Microsoft.

SANTA FE'S STATURE

Santa Fe has the highest elevation of any state capital—it's 7,000 feet above sea level. The highest point in the city is the capitol building, which is pretty appropriate!

"ONLY YOU!"

One of America's great celebrities got his start when he was rescued from a fire in Lincoln National Forest as a youngster in 1950. Who was it? Smokey Bear!

PREVENT SMOKEY FOREST FIRES

PARCHED PAVEMENT

Reportedly only one quarter of New Mexico's roads are paved. The climate is so dry that the parched earth creates "pavement" that's just as good as the real stuff!

BEEP, BEEP!

At 15 miles per hour, New Mexico's state bird, the roadrunner, is one of the fastest birds on the ground. It can catch—and eat—rattlesnakes, rodents, and scorpions!

DYNAMIC DUCKS

Deming hosts the annual Great American Duck Race. There are duck parades and pageants, tortilla tosses, spicy chili cook-offs, and even a crowning of a duck queen!

ALIEN INCIDENT

Interested in aliens? Roswell is your town! Visit the International UFO Museum and Research Center to learn about the 1947 "Roswell Incident," when a UFO reportedly crashed near the town.

PARDON THE INTERRUPTION

The government took over Los Alamos in 1947 for atomic research. The town began self-governance again in 1962, and the Los Alamos National Laboratory became a national historic landmark.

FLAG FACTS

New Mexico's flag sports an ancient sun symbol created by a Native America people called the Zia. The four sections symbolize the four main directions, the seasons, the parts of the day, and stages of life.

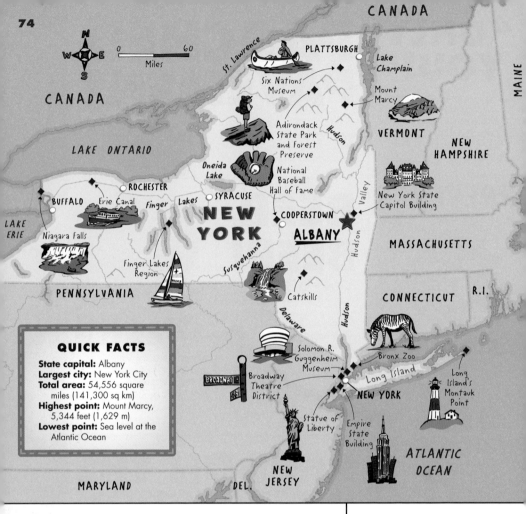

CANADA

CANADA

N W E S

0 — 60
Miles

St. Lawrence

PLATTSBURGH

Lake Champlain

Six Nations Museum

Mount Marcy

VERMONT

NEW HAMPSHIRE

Adirondack State Park and Forest Preserve

Hudson

LAKE ONTARIO

Oneida Lake

ROCHESTER

SYRACUSE

National Baseball Hall of Fame

New York State Capitol Building

BUFFALO

Erie Canal

Finger Lakes

NEW YORK

COOPERSTOWN

ALBANY

Valley

LAKE ERIE

Niagara Falls

Hudson

MASSACHUSETTS

Finger Lakes Region

Susquehanna

R.I.

CONNECTICUT

PENNSYLVANIA

Catskills

Delaware

Hudson

Bronx Zoo

Long Island

Long Island's Montauk Point

QUICK FACTS

State capital: Albany
Largest city: New York City
Total area: 54,556 square miles (141,300 sq km)
Highest point: Mount Marcy, 5,344 feet (1,629 m)
Lowest point: Sea level at the Atlantic Ocean

Solomon R. Guggenheim Museum

BROADWAY ST.

Broadway Theatre District

NEW YORK

Statue of Liberty

Empire State Building

ATLANTIC OCEAN

MARYLAND

DEL.

NEW JERSEY

MAINE

CANAL CELEBRATION

In 1825, "word" of the Erie Canal's completion traveled over 350 miles from Buffalo to New York City in just 81 minutes. How? The sounds of shots from cannons placed along the canal!

AMERICA'S DESSERT

Pearle Wait, a carpenter in LeRoy, revolutionized American desserts in 1897 by adding fruit flavoring to gelatin while trying to make cough medicine. His wife named the jiggly stuff Jell-O.

NYACK'S NIGHTHAWK

Edward Hopper, the artist behind the 1942 painting Nighthawks, hailed from Nyack. The haunting painting of customers in a diner late at night was inspired by an eatery in Manhattan.

BASEBALL BALONEY!

The Baseball Hall of Fame is located in Cooperstown, where Abner Doubleday was once rumored to have invented the game in 1839—even though he never made such claims himself.

FOUNDING FATHER'S TABLOID

The *New York Post* is one of the country's oldest newspapers. It was founded by Alexander Hamilton in 1801 in New York City.

LONG TIME COMING

Suffragettes gathered in Seneca Falls in 1848 for the first women's rights convention, to discuss winning the right to vote. Seventy-two years later, that right was finally granted.

IN A JAM

In 1848, Niagara Falls stopped flowing for 30 hours! Why? Ice floes from Lake Erie had jammed and blocked the water headed to the falls.

HAMILTON

UNUSUAL INAUGURATION

George Washington was inaugurated in New York City—at the time, the nation's capital—in 1789. He is the only president in history to take the oath in the Big Apple!

BETHEL-STOCK?

Contrary to popular belief, the three-day music festival known as Woodstock did not take place in Woodstock. It happened in Bethel in 1969, and half a million people were there!

ELEPHANT CROSSING

In 1884, after the Brooklyn Bridge was finished, P.T. Barnum led 21 circus elephants—including Jumbo!—across it in order to prove to the public that the bridge was safe.

Twenty One Elephants
AND STILL STANDING

NEW YORK

THE EMPIRE STATE

KENTUCKY

WEST VIRGINIA

VIRGINIA

D.C.

DELAWARE

University of North Carolina

North Carolina Museum of Life and Science

Wright Brothers National Memorial

Grandfather Mountain

Blue Ridge Parkway

International Civil Rights Center and Museum

Mount Mitchell State Park

Mountains

WINSTON-SALEM

GREENSBORO

DURHAM

North Carolina State Capitol

Roanoke

Tar

Albemarle Sound

TENNESSEE

Appalachian

ASHEVILLE

World's Largest Chest of Drawers

RALEIGH

North Carolina State Fair

NORTH CAROLINA

Pee Dee

CHARLOTTE

Neuse

Pamlico Sound

Outer Banks

North Carolina Apple Festival

Afro-American Cultural Center

National Hollerin' Contest

Cape Fear

WILMINGTON

Cape Hatteras National Seashore

SOUTH CAROLINA

GEORGIA

N W E S

0   50
Miles

QUICK FACTS

State capital: Raleigh
Largest city: Charlotte
Total area: 53,819 square miles (139,391 sq km)
Highest point: Mount Mitchell, 6,684 feet (2,037 m) in Yancey
Lowest point: Sea level along the Atlantic coast

USS North Carolina Battleship Memorial

ATLANTIC OCEAN

SLIP AND SLIDE

Sliding Rock is a 60-foot waterfall ending in a 7-foot-deep pool in Pisgah National Forest. The waterfall's slope is so gentle that people use it as a natural waterslide!

NASCAR LEGENDS

The only two drivers in the history of NASCAR to win seven championships are both from North Carolina: Richard Lee Petty of Level Cross and Dale Earnhardt of Kannaoplis.

DRAWERS GALORE

The "Home Furnishing Capital of the World." High Point is home to a 38-foot-tall Goddard-Townsend block front chest of drawers!

BLACKBEARD'S LAST SWIM

The pirate Blackbeard fought his last battle at Ocracoke in 1718. Legend says his headless body was thrown off a Naval ship, supposedly swimming around the ship three times before sinking!

PLANNING AHEAD

Chatham County is home to a military bunker several stories below ground, known as the Big Hole. Its purpose? To maintain communications in the event of a nuclear attack. (How cheerful—*not*!)

FANCY FORKS

At a typical 8-course dinner at the Biltmore House—the 250-room Vanderbilt mansion completed in 1895 in Asheville—guests used 15 different pieces of sterling silver utensils.

ART FOR ALL

In 1947, North Carolina became the first state to use public funds to purchase an art collection. You can see the collection at the North Carolina Museum of Art—for free!

DEMAND FOR DONUTS

When Vernon Rudolph started Krispy Kreme in 1937 in Old Salem, he had to cut a hole in the bakery wall to accommodate the many customers demanding his delicious donuts!

Even after he'd made it big, basketball great Michael Jordan of Wilmington used to wear his University of North Carolina shorts under his Chicago Bulls uniform for good luck.

SUPER SHORTS

DARE TO DISAPPEAR

In 1587, Virginia Dare of Roanoke became the first English child born in North America. But no one knows what happened to her or the other colonists. They simply disappeared.

NORTH CAROLINA THE TAR HEEL STATE

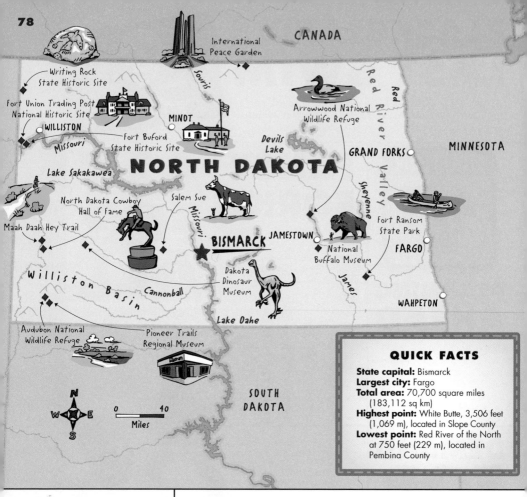

CANADA

International Peace Garden

Writing Rock State Historic Site

Fort Union Trading Post National Historic Site

WILLISTON

Missouri

MINOT

Fort Buford State Historic Site

Devils Lake

Arrowwood National Wildlife Refuge

GRAND FORKS

MINNESOTA

Red River Valley

Souris

Sheyenne

Lake Sakakawea

NORTH DAKOTA

North Dakota Cowboy Hall of Fame

Salem Sue

Maah Daah Hey Trail

Missouri

BISMARCK

JAMESTOWN

National Buffalo Museum

Fort Ransom State Park

FARGO

Williston Basin

Cannonball

Dakota Dinosaur Museum

James

WAHPETON

Lake Oahe

Audubon National Wildlife Refuge

Pioneer Trails Regional Museum

SOUTH DAKOTA

N W E S

0   40
Miles

QUICK FACTS

State capital: Bismarck
Largest city: Fargo
Total area: 70,700 square miles (183,112 sq km)
Highest point: White Butte, 3,506 feet (1,069 m), located in Slope County
Lowest point: Red River of the North at 750 feet (229 m), located in Pembina County

GOBBLE, GOBBLE

Every summer since the early 1960s, Aneta has hosted what they call the world's largest turkey barbeque. The event attracts thousands of people, and they barbeque close to 300 turkeys!

GIVE
PEACE A CHANCE

The International Peace Garden straddles the boundary between North Dakota and the Canadian province of Manitoba. It features a floral clock and a memorial to those who lost their lives on 9/11.

TREMENDOUS TV ANTENNA

At 2,063 feet, the KVLY-TV Tower near Galesburg is the tallest structure in North America! (The only human-made structure that's taller is the Burj Dubai, in the United Arab Emirates.)

BUFFALO CITY

Jamestown, known as Buffalo City, has been home to a 26-foot-tall, 46-foot-long, 60-ton sculpture of a buffalo since 1959. It also has a (real!) albino buffalo named Dakota Miracle.

CENTRAL NORTH AMERICA

In 1931, Rugby was declared the geographical center of North America and honored with a pyramid-shaped monument. The town's unofficial motto is, fittingly, "Welcome to the center of it all!"

THE NAME GAME

In 1947, and again in 1989, the state legislature struck down a proposed resolution to strike the word "North" from North Dakota. For now, "Dakota" is just a nickname . . .

NORDIC CELEBRATION

Do not confuse the Horse Fest with Minot's Høstfest, North America's largest Scandinavian festival featuring Nordic cuisine (lutefisk, also known as fish in lye!) and clothing (clogs!).

A FLIGHT FIRST

In 1928, Carl Ben Eielson of Hatton was the first person to fly a plane across the Arctic Ocean. The flight took a grueling 20 hours!

UNFAIRLY NAMED!

Devils Lake was actually named Spirit Lake by the Sioux Indians, but white settlers mistranslated the name. The "evil" name stuck, owing to legends of monsters in the lake.

HORSING AROUND

The Taylor Horse Fest attracts close to 6,000 people each July and features just about every kind of horse event you can think of . . . including a Horse Fest musical!

NORTH DAKOTA THE PEACE GARDEN STATE

CANADA

MICHIGAN

LAKE ERIE

Marblehead Lighthouse

TOLEDO

Maumee

Rock and Roll Hall of Fame

SANDUSKY

CLEVELAND

Cuyahoga

American Civil War Museum of Ohio

African Safari Wildlife Park

Sandusky

Cedar Point Amusement Park

YOUNGSTOWN

PENNSYLVANIA

Edison Birthplace Museum

AKRON

Neil Armstrong Air & Space Museum

Scioto

CANTON

Pro Football Hall of Fame

OHIO

Wyandot Popcorn Museum

Schoenbrunn Village State Memorial

Appalachian Plateau

INDIANA

Ohio Statehouse

SunWatch Indian Village/ Archaeological Park

Muskingum

Ohio

DAYTON

The Horseshoe, Ohio State University

COLUMBUS

Great Miami

Scioto

Hocking Hills State Park

WEST VIRGINIA

Cincinnati Zoo & Botanical Garden

CINCINNATI

Ohio

KENTUCKY

N W E S

0   30
Miles

QUICK FACTS

State capital: Columbus
Largest city: Columbus
Total area: 44,825 square miles (116,096 sq km)
Highest point: Campbell Hill, 1,550 feet (472 m), located in Logan County
Lowest point: Ohio River, 455 feet (139 m), located in Hamilton County

A DRAWING DELIGHT

Bryan is home to the Ohio Art Company, which manufactures one of the most popular and creative toys invented in the 20th century—the Etch A Sketch!

EXTRAORDINARY ELECTION

Cleveland elected the first African American mayor of a major city in 1967. Carl B. Stokes became mayor after graduating from law school and serving three terms in the Ohio legislature.

ROLLER COASTER MANIA

Cedar Point Amusement Park in Sandusky has 17 roller coasters—that's more than any other park. Pay a visit and ride the Mean Streak, one of the steepest roller coasters in the world!

OHIO

COWABUNGA!

Nancy Cartwright, the voice of Bart Simpson, was born in Kettering. Yes, you read that right—a woman provides the voice of *The Simpsons*'s famous fourth-grade troublemaker!

BIRTHPLACE OF PRESIDENTS

Seven U.S. presidents were born in Ohio! Ulysses Grant, Rutherford Hayes, James Garfield, Benjamin Harrison, William McKinley, William Taft, and Warren Harding dominated the White House from 1869 to 1923.

FUNKY FLAG

Ohio is the only state with a flag that is not rectangular. It is a burgee, or "swallowtail" design, which looks like a forked pennant.

PERFECT PITCH

The best pitchers in major league baseball are given the Cy Young Award, named after a brilliant pitcher from Gilmore who retired in 1911 after winning 511 games!

SCARY SCHOOL!

Margaret Hamilton, also known as the Wicked Witch of the West in *The Wizard of Oz*, ran a Cleveland nursery school before becoming an actress. Hopefully she was nicer as Ms. Hamilton!

DOUBLE TAKE

The Twin Days Festival takes place in Twinsburg, naturally. Every August, nearly 3,000 sets of twins take part in sports events, barbeques, and the "Double Take" Parade.

MAN OF TOMORROW

Created by Jerry Siegel and Joe Shuster of Cleveland, Superman first appeared in the early 1930s. Siegel and Shuster sold the Man of Steel to Detective Comics and he took off faster than a speeding bullet!

THE BUCKEYE STATE

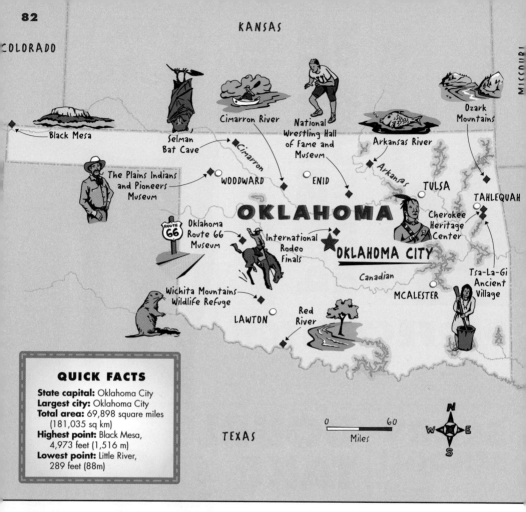

COLORADO
KANSAS
MISSOURI

Black Mesa

Cimarron River

Selman Bat Cave

Cimarron

National Wrestling Hall of Fame and Museum

Arkansas River

Arkansas

Ozark Mountains

The Plains Indians and Pioneers Museum

WOODWARD

ENID

TULSA

TAHLEQUAH

OKLAHOMA

Cherokee Heritage Center

ROUTE 66

Oklahoma Route 66 Museum

International Rodeo Finals

★ **OKLAHOMA CITY**

Canadian

Tsa-La-Gi Ancient Village

Wichita Mountains Wildlife Refuge

MCALESTER

LAWTON

Red River

QUICK FACTS

State capital: Oklahoma City
Largest city: Oklahoma City
Total area: 69,898 square miles (181,035 sq km)
Highest point: Black Mesa, 4,973 feet (1,516 m)
Lowest point: Little River, 289 feet (88m)

TEXAS

0   60
Miles

N
W   E
S

SOONER STATE

Where does Oklahoma's nickname, "The Sooner State," come from? In 1889, some white settlers staked their claims to land before, or "sooner," than they were supposed to.

OILY CAPITOL BUILDING

The state capitol in Oklahoma City produces more than just legislation—it also produces oil! The building sits atop the active oil wells of the Oklahoma City Oil Field.

GREAT SEAL OF THE STATE OF OKLAHOMA

1907

THOR RELOCATES

Marvel Comics hero Thor has left the Big Apple for Oklahoma! The new writer of the series decided to set Thor's stories near the ancient Heavener Runestone, in Heavener.

PARKING PAIN

When you put a quarter in a parking meter, thank Carl C. Magee of Oklahoma City. He invented the device in 1935, much to the chagrin of drivers everywhere!

COW CHIP CHAMPS

Each spring, the panhandle city of Beaver holds the World Championship Cow Chip Throw! The town's mascot is King Cow Chip, a mound of cow poop wearing a crown.

INDIAN NATION

Oklahoma is home to more American Indian tribes than any other state. In fact, the word "Oklahoma" comes from two Choctaw words that translate as "red people."

WATER POWER

The Pensacola Dam in Grand Lake is the largest multiple arch dam in the world. The 5,145-foot dam has 51 arches and provides power for 24 counties in Oklahoma.

Who bombed Boise City during World War II? Oops! The U.S. military accidentally dropped six practice bombs full of sand on the town in 1943. No one was hurt.

BOMB BLUNDER

PITT STOP

Brad Pitt, the actor known for his roles in *Thelma & Louise*, *Interview with the Vampire*, and *Babel*, was born William Bradley Pitt in Shawnee in 1963.

Sylvan Goldman of Oklahoma City invented the shopping cart in 1937. Everyone rejected the carts until he paid young people in good shape to use them. Then they took off!

CART CRAZE

WASHINGTON

Lewis and Clark Campsite

Columbia River Maritime Museum

ASTORIA

World Forestry Center

Mount Hood Railroad

Columbia

PORTLAND

PACIFIC OCEAN

Tamastslikt Cultural Institute

Snake

SALEM

Mission Mill Museum

John Day Fossil Beds National Monument

John Day

IDAHO

Yaquina Head Lighthouse

Coast Range

Willamette

Cascade Mountains

Deschutes

OREGON

ONTARIO

EUGENE

BEND

National Historic Oregon Trail Interpretive Center

Museum of Natural and Cultural History

Newberry National Volcanic Monument

COOS BAY

Oregon Dunes National Recreation Area

Crater Lake

Oregon Shakespeare Festival

Great Basin

N
W E
S

0   50
Miles

Rogue

MEDFORD

Klamath

KLAMATH FALLS

Oregon Caves National Monument

CALIFORNIA

NEVADA

QUICK FACTS

State capital: Salem
Largest city: Portland
Total area: 98,381 square miles (254,807 sq km)
Highest point: Mount Hood, 11,239 feet (3,426 m)
Lowest point: Sea level along the Pacific Ocean

MARBLE CONSISTENCY

The caves at the Oregon Caves National Monument in the Siskiyou Mountains were discovered in 1874. They are natural marble, which keeps the temperature at 44°F year round.

PACHYDERM PROOF

The John Day Fossil Beds in Kimberly are home to some of the world's oldest fossils of the early rhinoceros, an animal that resembled a horse more than today's rhinoceros.

SHORT COMPETITION

The 120-foot D River in Lincoln used to compete with Montana's Roe River to be the "shortest river in the world," a distinction *Guinness World Records* no longer recognizes.

BEING BORING

There is a town in Oregon called Boring. Visitors entering the town are greeted by a sign that says, "Entering Boring." And what's their motto? "Boring—the most exciting place to live!"

STRANGE STANDARD

Unlike any other state flag, the Oregon state flag is double-sided! The front sports the state seal, and the back pictures the state animal, the beaver.

FABULOUS FLOP

Portland-born track star Dick Fosbury won Olympic gold in 1968 by going over the high jump head first and backwards. This now-common method is called the "Fosbury flop"!

MARKETING MAKEOVER

Oregon grows 99% of the entire U.S. commercial crop of filberts. Don't know what a filbert is? You do, actually—"filbert" is just a less glamorous term for "hazelnut"!

DEEP WATERS

Crater Lake National Park is home to the deepest lake in the United States. Crater Lake is more than 1,900 feet deep, and was created when a volcano erupted and collapsed 7,700 years ago!

A TOSS-UP

The name of Oregon's capital in 1851—Portland—was decided in a coin toss when the city founders both wanted to name the city after their hometowns (Boston, Massachusetts, and Portland, Maine).

The world's oldest sandals were found in 1938 by a University of Oregon archaeologist in a cave at Fort Rock. The 10,000-year-old shoes are made of sagebrush bark.

ANCIENT FLIP-FLOPS

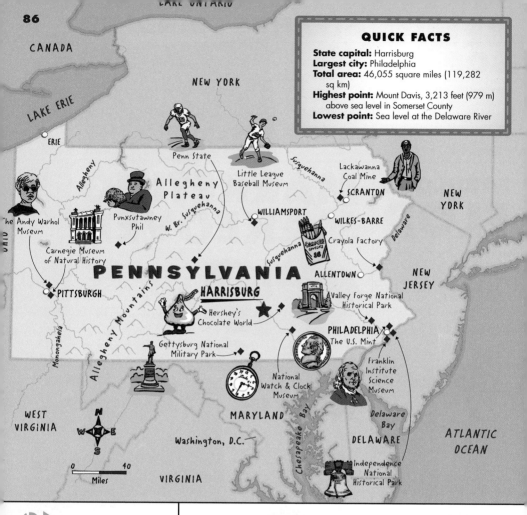

LAKE ONTARIO

CANADA

LAKE ERIE

NEW YORK

ERIE

QUICK FACTS

State capital: Harrisburg
Largest city: Philadelphia
Total area: 46,055 square miles (119,282 sq km)
Highest point: Mount Davis, 3,213 feet (979 m) above sea level in Somerset County
Lowest point: Sea level at the Delaware River

Penn State

Allegheny

Allegheny Plateau

Susquehanna

Little League Baseball Museum

Lackawanna Coal Mine

SCRANTON

NEW YORK

The Andy Warhol Museum

Punxsutawney Phil

W. Br. Susquehanna

WILLIAMSPORT

WILKES-BARRE

Delaware

Crayola Factory

Carnegie Museum of Natural History

Susquehanna

PENNSYLVANIA

ALLENTOWN

NEW JERSEY

PITTSBURGH

Allegheny Mountains

HARRISBURG

Hershey's Chocolate World

Valley Forge National Historical Park

OHIO

Monongahela

Gettysburg National Military Park

National Watch & Clock Museum

PHILADELPHIA
The U.S. Mint

Franklin Institute Science Museum

WEST VIRGINIA

N W E S

MARYLAND

Delaware Bay

DELAWARE

ATLANTIC OCEAN

0   40
Miles

Washington, D.C.

Chesapeake Bay

Independence National Historical Park

VIRGINIA

GROUNDHOG DAY

Punxsutawney is home to Phil, the legendary groundhog who leaves his burrow on February 2 and "predicts" how much longer winter will last. He made his first observance in 1886.

WHERE'S THE "H"?

In 1890, the United States Postal Office dropped the "h" in "Pittsburgh." Concerned citizens mounted an effort to get their "h" back and it was officially restored in 1911.

MEETING THE ENEMY

Commodore Oliver Hazard Perry defeated the British on Lake Erie during the War of 1812, reporting his victory with the words, "We have met the enemy and they are ours!"

PHILLY LOVES PRETZELS

The average Philadelphian eats over 20 pounds of soft pretzels per year! (To give you an idea of how much Philly loves pretzels, the average American eats two pounds per year.)

SHORT SPEECH

President Abraham Lincoln's famous Gettysburg Address in Gettysburg is one of the most quoted political speeches in history—and also one of the shortest. It was just over two minutes long.

FLEXIBLE ARTIST

The artist N.C. Wyeth of Chadds Ford illustrated the children's classic *Treasure Island* as well as ads for Cream of Wheat and Coca-Cola. (Artists have to eat, too, you know!)

MONUMENT TO BEN

In Philadelphia, a 101-foot-tall, 60-ton sculpture of a lightning strike, a kite, and a key commemorates Ben Franklin's experiment that forever changed our understanding of electricity.

YUMMY COLORS

Take a tour of the Crayola Crayon factory in Easton and learn how wax and pigment combine to make colors like macaroni and cheese, mango tango, and jazzberry jam.

IT'S THE REFRESHING THING TO DO

Jim Thorpe of Carlisle, arguably the greatest athlete of the 20th century, played professional baseball, won two events at the 1912 Olympics, and was a high school football star.

AMAZING ATHLETE

PENNSYLVANIA
THE KEYSTONE STATE

MILLIONS OF KISSES

Factories in Hershey, also known as the "Sweetest Place on Earth," produce 80 million chocolate Kisses a day. How many do you think you could eat in one sitting?

ATLANTIC OCEAN

Arecibo Observatory

Arecibo Lighthouse and Historical Park

San Cristóbal Fort

SAN JUAN

El Yunque National Forest

Caguana Indian Ceremonial Park

ARECIBO

BAYAMÓN

CAROLINA

Culebra Island

Manatí

La Plata

Loíza

Añasco

Arecibo

PUERTO RICO

Mona Passage

MAYAGÜEZ

Tres Picachos

Cordillera Central

CAGUAS

Vieques Passage

Vieques Sound

Vieques Island

PONCE

Cartagena Lagoon Natural Reserve

Caja de Muertos

Parque de Las Ciencias Luis A. Ferré

Las Cabezas de San Juan State Park

Cabo Rojo Lighthouse

Ponce Museum of Art

CARIBBEAN SEA

0   20
Miles

WHO WAS FIRST?

Long before the Spanish or the Americans showed up, Puerto Rico belonged to the Taíno Indians, and was called Borinquén, which means the "Land of the Mighty Lord."

VOTING RESTRICTIONS

Puerto Ricans have been U.S. citizens since 1917. However, they can vote in presidential elections only if they reside in one of the 50 states.

Puerto Rico is one of the most densely populated islands on the planet. With a population of close to 4 million, there are 1,000 people per square mile!

CLOSE QUARTERS

BIT OF BACKGROUND

The island of Puerto Rico was ceded to the U.S. by Spain in 1898, after the Spanish-American War. In 1952, Puerto Rico became a self-governing territory of the U.S.

AWARDS APLENTY

Rita Moreno of Humacao was the only Hispanic woman to win an Emmy, a Tony, an Oscar, and a Grammy. This great talent was on Broadway by the time she was 13!

TOP TELESCOPE

The Arecibo Observatory, near Arecibo, has the biggest radio telescope in the world. Scientists and students from all over use the telescope for planetary—and extraterrestrial—research.

THE OLD CITY

San Juan, Puerto Rico's capital, has some of the first forts ever built by the Spanish in the Americas, and the oldest parts of the city still have original cobblestone streets.

TREE WONDERLAND

El Yunque National Forest is the only tropical forest in the national forest system. It has 240 species of trees, 23 of which are only found in El Yunque!

There are nearly a million Puerto Ricans in New York, many of whom consider themselves Nuyorican, a name that combines "Puerto Rican" and "New York."

NUYORICAN PRIDE

HEART OF GOLD

Baseball legend Roberto Clemente of Barrio San Antón played for the Brooklyn Dodgers and Pittsburgh Pirates before dying in a 1972 plane crash while bringing aid to Nicaraguan earthquake victims.

Blackstone River Rapids

WOONSOCKET

Slater Mill

Seagrave Memorial Observatory

Chepachet

Blackstone

Jerimoth Hill

Rhode Island School of Design Museum

PROVIDENCE

SCITUATE

PAWTUCKET

Crescent Park Carousel

Roger Williams Park Zoo

Conimicut Point Park

Pawtuxet

MASSACHUSETTS

New England Wireless and Steam Museum

WARWICK

Providence

Coggeshall Farm Museum

BRISTOL

Herreshoff Marine Museum

RHODE ISLAND

Narragansett Bay

Sakonnet

Rhode Island

Newport Butterfly Zoo

CONNECTICUT

Wood

Quonset Air Museum

NEWPORT

Rhode Island Sound

Pawcatuck

CHARLESTOWN

Rose Island Lighthouse

New England Aquarium Exploration Center

WESTERLY

Block Island Sound

ATLANTIC OCEAN

Block Island

0   10
Miles

QUICK FACTS

State capital: Providence
Largest city: Providence
Total area: 1,545 square miles
(4,002 sq km)
Highest point: Jerimoth Hill,
812 feet (247 m) above sea level
Lowest point: Sea level along
the Atlantic Ocean

ROLL ON!

In the summer of 1866, a roller-skating club built the country's first public skating rink in a Newport hotel, and vacationers went crazy over the latest fad on wheels!

SMALLEST STATE?

Though it is the smallest state in the nation, Rhode Island consists of 36 islands as well as mainland, and has over 400 miles of coastline.

RIVER MIGHT

In 1789 on the Blackstone River in Pawtucket, Samuel Slater, aka the "Father of the American Industrial Revolution," designed and built the first American textile mill powered by water.

WELL-DRESSED TERMITE

Nibbles Woodaway is a 58-foot-long hurricane-proof blue termite who lives on top of New England Pest Control in Providence—and who dresses appropriately for the holidays!

TEMPLE IN DISGUISE

In 1776 in Newport, the British used Touro Synagogue—the oldest temple in America—as a hospital, in order to ensure its survival during the Revolutionary War.

RHODE WHAT?!

Rhode Island isn't officially called Rhode Island. The state's full name is "The State of Rhode Island and Providence Plantations." (The latter refers to the mainland part of the state.)

FAMOUS FOURTH FEST

Bristol is home to one of the oldest 4th of July parades in the nation, first held in 1785. A red, white, and blue stripe on the town's main street marks the parade route year round.

FACIAL HAIR FAME

Ambrose Burnside, the Civil War general who commanded Fort Adams in Newport, was famous for his facial hair. Barbers called his odd bristles "burnsides," and later, "sideburns."

MOVE OVER, PONY

America's first auto race on a track took place at the Narragansett Trotting Park in Cranston, in 1896. Just imagine how confused the horses must have been!

"UNDERDOG IS HERE!"

Providence is proud to call Underdog its own. The 2007 movie, *Underdog*, about a dog with super powers (and a fancy cape) was shot in over a dozen locations around town.

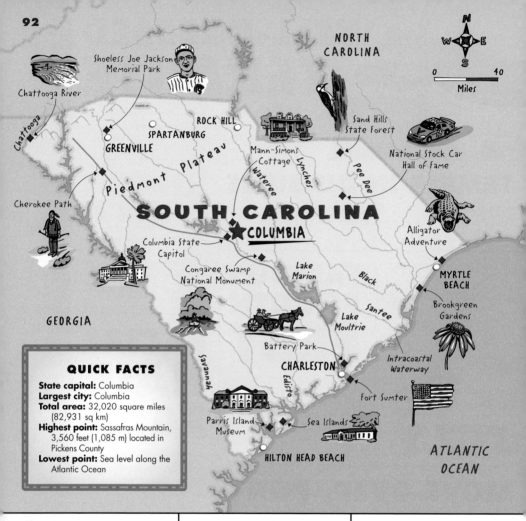

NORTH CAROLINA

Chattooga River

Shoeless Joe Jackson Memorial Park

Chattooga

ROCK HILL

SPARTANBURG

GREENVILLE

Sand Hills State Forest

National Stock Car Hall of Fame

Piedmont Plateau

Mann-Simons Cottage

Wateree

Lynches

Pee Dee

Cherokee Path

SOUTH CAROLINA

★ **COLUMBIA**

Columbia State Capitol

Alligator Adventure

Congaree Swamp National Monument

Lake Marion

Black

MYRTLE BEACH

Brookgreen Gardens

GEORGIA

Lake Moultrie

Santee

Battery Park

CHARLESTON

Intracoastal Waterway

Edisto

Fort Sumter

Parris Island Museum

Sea Islands

ATLANTIC OCEAN

HILTON HEAD BEACH

N W E S

0 — 40 Miles

QUICK FACTS

State capital: Columbia
Largest city: Columbia
Total area: 32,020 square miles (82,931 sq km)
Highest point: Sassafras Mountain, 3,560 feet (1,085 m) located in Pickens County
Lowest point: Sea level along the Atlantic Ocean

SOUTHERN PEACH CAPITOL

The one-million-gallon Peachoid Water Tower in Gaffney attempts to set the record straight about exactly who produces the most peaches in the South. (It's South Carolina, not Georgia.)

WHAT'S RETIREMENT?

U.S. Senator Strom Thurmond of Edgefield left office in 2003, when he was 100 years old, making him the longest-serving senator in U.S. history.

THAT CHARLESTON STYLE

The Charleston, the dance craze of the 1920s popularized by flappers, was believed to have been created around 1900 by African Americans living off the coast of—you guessed it—Charleston.

THE FIRST SHOT

The Civil War began on April 12, 1861, at Fort Sumter in Charleston Harbor. Confederate forces fired the first shot and won the fort, holding on to it for four years.

PUTT-PUTT CHAMPS

Myrtle Beach has the most miniature golf courses in the United States (over 40). Not surprisingly, it also hosts the Masters National Pro Mini Golf Championship!

FIELD OF HISTORY

Spartanburg is home to the country's oldest minor league baseball stadium, Duncan Park, which hosted its first game in 1926. Locals are currently trying to save the park from disrepair.

ONE GIANT STEP

In 1999, Nancy Ruth Mace of Goose Creek became the first woman to graduate from The Citadel, one of the country's premier military colleges, ending 150 years of single-gender education there.

SAVE THE FLYTRAP!

The Venus Flytrap, a carnivorous plant native to South Carolina that actually catches its prey and digests it, is disappearing, owing to land development and encroaching humans.

Frogmore Stew, named after a fishing town near Beaufort, is a one-pot, boiled meal of shrimp, crab, and corn, traditionally served on newspaper! (There are no frogs involved.)

LOWCOUNTRY BOIL!

James Brown, the Barnwell-born singer who was inducted into the Rock and Roll Hall of Fame in 1986, was called the "Godfather of Soul" and "Soul Brother Number One."

"I FEEL GOOD!"

SOUTH CAROLINA

THE PALMETTO STATE

NORTH DAKOTA

MINNESOTA

Fort Sisseton State Historical Park

Motorcycle Museum & Hall of Fame

Grand

Moreau

Missouri

ABERDEEN

WATERTOWN

South Dakota Air and Space Museum

Great Lake Dahe Plains

SOUTH DAKOTA

South Dakota Art Museum

Big Sioux

Black Hills National Forest

Cheyenne

PIERRE

South Dakota State Capitol

James

RAPID CITY

Mount Rushmore

CHAMBERLAIN

Great Plains Zoo

Custer State Park

White

Akta Lakota Museum & Cultural Center

SIOUX FALLS

Badlands National Park

Missouri

South Dakota Hall of Fame

YANKTON

IOWA

Jewel Cave National Monument

Sitting Bull and Sacagawea Monuments

USS South Dakota Battleship Memorial

NEBRASKA

QUICK FACTS

State capital: Pierre
Largest city: Sioux Falls
Total area: 77,117 square miles (199,731 sq km)
Highest point: Harney Peak, 7,242 feet (2,207 m), in Pennington County
Lowest point: Big Stone Lake, 966 feet (294 m), in Roberts County

N W E S

0   40
Miles

FAMOUS FACE

Tom Brokaw grew up in Yankton, graduated from the University of South Dakota, and went on to become one of our nation's most famous network news anchors.

MOTORCYCLE MADNESS

Every August, the population of Spearfish explodes when motorcyclists from all over the country arrive for the Sturgis Rally, started in 1938, which features races and road tours.

DANCES WITH OSCAR

The movie *Dances With Wolves*, which won seven Oscars in 1990 and tells the story of a U.S. lieutenant who befriends Sioux Indians, was filmed primarily in the Black Hills.

FIERY FOUNTAIN

The Flaming Fountain in Pierre is exactly what it sounds like—a fountain on fire! It's fed by natural gas and looks beautiful, but smells bad!

ACCURATE TRANSLATION

Badlands National Park derived its name from the Lakota Indians, who called the area *mako sica*, meaning, "land bad." Its desolate beauty pretty much speaks for itself.

SIZEABLE SCULPTURE

When it is finished, the 563-foot-tall Black Hills monument to Crazy Horse—the Indian leader who fought at the Battle of Little Big Horn—will surpass Mount Rushmore as the largest sculpture in the world.

PRESIDENTIAL CRANIUMS

President's Park, in Lead, features giant, 16- to 20-foot-tall busts of all the U.S. presidents arranged in chronological order. (George Washington—Mr. Number One—gets a view of the snack bar.)

LAWLESS LAWMAN

Wild Bill Hickok, a lawman with a criminal record, was killed in 1876 in Deadwood when he broke his own rule and played poker in a chair that didn't face the door.

PIONEER GIRL

In *Little Town on the Prairie*, part of her Little House series, Laura Ingalls Wilder wrote about pioneer life in DeSmet.

CORN ART

Mitchell is home to the famous Corn Palace, which dates to 1892. The palace is redecorated each year with new murals of life in South Dakota—made out of corn!

MITCHELL CORN PALACE

SOUTH DAKOTA

THE MOUNT RUSHMORE STATE

OHIO

ILLINOIS

INDIANA

WEST VIRGINIA

KENTUCKY

World's Largest Guitar

Bristol Motor Speedway

MISSOURI

VIRGINIA

Tennessee National Wildlife Refuge

Country Music Hall of Fame and Museum

Knoxville Zoo

NASHVILLE Cumberland

Musicians Hall of Fame and Museum

KNOXVILLE

Appalachian Mountains

NORTH CAROLINA

ARKANSAS

Mississippi

Tennessee State Capitol

TENNESSEE

Tennessee

Great Smoky Mountains National Park

Cumberland Caverns

Tennessee

MEMPHIS

Elvis Presley's Graceland

Sharpe Planetarium

CHATTANOOGA

Creative Discovery Museum

NASCAR SpeedPark

SOUTH CAROLINA

MISSISSIPPI

ALABAMA

GEORGIA

N W E S

0   50
Miles

QUICK FACTS

State capital: Nashville
Largest city: Memphis
Total area: 42,143 square miles (109,151 sq km)
Highest point: Clingmans Dome, 6,643 feet (2,025 m), located in Sevier County
Lowest point: Mississippi River in Shelby County, 178 feet (54 m)

THE KING'S HOUSE

Graceland, the Memphis home of Elvis Presley, is visited by about 600,000 people a year. The only home with more visitors per year is the White House!

"BE A GOOD BOY!"

A woman's right to vote hinged on one man in 1920: Tennessee representative Harry Burn. He planned to vote against suffrage, but a note from his mother changed his mind.

STRIKE THREE

In 1931, 17-year-old Jackie Mitchell of the Chattanooga Lookouts struck out Babe Ruth and Lou Gehrig during an exhibition game against the Yankees. *She* was fired a few days later.

THE VOLUNTEER STATE

Tennessee earned its nickname during the War of 1812, when volunteer soldiers from Tennessee served valiantly under General Andrew Jackson at the Battle of New Orleans.

A PIECE OF GREECE

Greece in Nashville? Yup! A full-scale homage to the Parthenon in Athens was built for Tennessee's 1897 Centennial Exposition as a monument to classic architecture.

INTERESTING CHOICE

Even though the country-gospel group the Oak Ridge Boys was based in Knoxville, they took their name from nearby Oak Ridge, where the atomic bomb was being developed.

PARADING DUCKS

The Peabody Memphis hotel features the Duck March, during which ducks parade through the lobby to the Peabody fountain daily. (Duck is not on the menu at the hotel.)

SHORT BUT SWEET

The Bristol Motor Speedway is only half a mile long—but it's known as the World's Fastest Half Mile. Racing on it has been compared to "flying fighter jets in a gymnasium."

WHAT A VIEW!

On a clear day, Tennesseans say you can see seven states from the top of Chattanooga's Lookout Mountain: Tennessee, Georgia, Kentucky, Virginia, North Carolina, South Carolina, and Alabama.

COUNTRY MUSIC GOLDMINE

The Grand Ole Opry, the nation's longest-running live radio broadcast, has been on the air since 1925.

QUICK FACTS

State capital: Austin
Largest city: Houston
Total area: 268,581 square
miles (695,625 sq km)
Highest point: Guadalupe Peak,
8,749 feet (2,667 m)
Lowest point: Sea level along
the Gulf of Mexico

PROPER CHILI

Texans are fond of saying, "If you know beans about chili, you know chili ain't got no beans." Texans put beef and tomatoes in their chili, and leave the beans for burritos.

INFURIATING ARTIST?

Robert Rauschenberg, born in Port Arthur in 1925, was famous for paintings called "Singular Forms," featuring one solid color on a canvas. The paintings continue to infuriate—and enrapture—today.

AVIATRICES, UNITE!

Avenger Field in Sweetwater was an airbase for female pilots in World War II. From 1943 to 1944, the base contained the only military flight school for women in the world.

SO MANY COWS!

Texas has 14 million cattle. To give you an idea of exactly what that means, 46 states have fewer people than Texas has cattle. (How many cow chips do they have?!)

FROM BIG TO BOLD

When Alaska became a state in 1959, Texas had to change "largest" to "boldest" in its state song. (Texas is over 268,000 square miles; Alaska is over 663,000 square miles.)

Space Center Houston, the visitors' center at NASA's Johnson Space Center, is home to the Blast Off Theater, which allows visitors to experience a simulated space launch—complete with billowing smoke!

BLAST OFF!

INSPIRED BY A KINGDOM

Think the buildings at the University of Texas at El Paso look like the mountain kingdom of Bhutan? You're right! The university's architecture is modeled after Bhutanese monasteries.

SPELLING OUTLAW

Bonnie Parker was the Dallas citywide spelling bee champion before she fell in love with Clyde Barrow in 1930 and became half of the infamous outlaw duo Bonnie & Clyde.

GRAND OLD FLAG(S)

The flags of France, Spain, Mexico, the Republic of Texas, the Confederate States of America, and the United States have all flown over Texas at least once since 1685.

HORRIBLE HURRICANE

The Galveston hurricane of 1900 was the deadliest natural disaster in U.S. history. Over 5,000 people died in the raging storm and almost the entire city was destroyed.

THE LONE STAR STATE

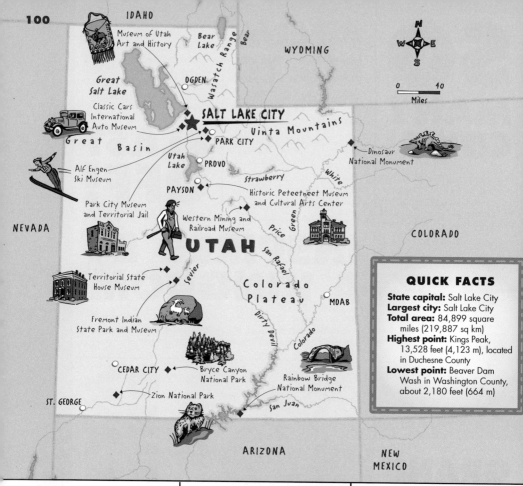

IDAHO

WYOMING

Museum of Utah Art and History

Bear Lake

Bear

Wasatch Range

Great Salt Lake

OGDEN

SALT LAKE CITY

Uinta Mountains

Classic Cars International Auto Museum

PARK CITY

Dinosaur National Monument

Great Basin

Utah Lake

PROVO

White

Alf Engen Ski Museum

Strawberry

Green

PAYSON

Historic Peteetneet Museum and Cultural Arts Center

Park City Museum and Territorial Jail

Western Mining and Railroad Museum

Price

San Rafael

COLORADO

NEVADA

UTAH

Sevier

Territorial State House Museum

Colorado Plateau

MOAB

Fremont Indian State Park and Museum

Dirty Devil

Colorado

CEDAR CITY

Bryce Canyon National Park

Rainbow Bridge National Monument

ST. GEORGE

Zion National Park

San Juan

ARIZONA

NEW MEXICO

N W E S

0   40
Miles

QUICK FACTS

State capital: Salt Lake City
Largest city: Salt Lake City
Total area: 84,899 square miles (219,887 sq km)
Highest point: Kings Peak, 13,528 feet (4,123 m), located in Duchesne County
Lowest point: Beaver Dam Wash in Washington County, about 2,180 feet (664 m)

AN OUTLAW IS BORN

Robert Leroy Parker, born in 1866 in Beaver, changed his name to Butch Cassidy after he worked as a butcher. He chose "Cassidy" to honor his criminal mentor, Mike Cassidy.

SPEEDING ON SALT

Speed racers of all kinds travel to the Bonneville Salt Flats, one of the flattest places on earth, to race. Hundreds of land speed records have been set—and broken—there!

LA LA LAAAAA!

The world-famous and Grammy Award-winning Mormon Tabernacle Choir, based in Salt Lake City, was founded in 1847. The 360-member choir has sung at five presidential inaugurations.

STONE RAINBOW

Lake Powell is home to Rainbow Bridge, a 290-foot-high natural stone arch formed over a creek. The Navajo call the arch "Nonnezoshe," which means "rainbow turned to stone."

BELLYBUTTON TOWN

Levan is in the center of Utah. Since "Levan" spells "navel" backward, some suspect that whoever named the town had a good sense of humor. (Or a knack for coincidences.)

GREEN JELL-O SALAD

If you're a fan of Jell-O, Utah is the place for you. Green Jell-O salad is a staple in Utah, some versions of which include pineapple, cream cheese, and Sprite. (Gulp.)

DINO LOVER'S DELIGHT

Dinosaur National Monument near Vernal is home to the Dinosaur Quarry, a steep wall of rock that contains over 1,500 dinosaur bones, some of which are still in skeleton form.

RAILROAD'S GOLDEN MOMENT

In May of 1869 at Promontory Summit, a golden spike was used to symbolically join the Union Pacific and Central Pacific lines, forming America's first trans-continental railroad.

Vernal
UTAH'S DINOSAUR LAND

119

DIGGING IN

According to NASA, the Bingham Canyon Open Pit Copper Mine in Salt Lake Valley is one of the largest holes ever dug by humans. It is almost a mile deep and 2.5 miles wide.

THELMA & LOUISE

Dead Horse Point National Park doubles as the Grand Canyon in the final scene of the 1991 Oscar-winning film *Thelma & Louise* when the women drive their convertible off a cliff.

CANADA

Lake Memphremagog

Abenaki Tribal Museum

Herrmann's Royal Lipizzan Stallions

Vermont Maple Festival

Lamoille

Smugglers' Notch

Connecticut

ST. JOHNSBURY

MAINE

Underwater Shipwrecks

Lake Champlain

BURLINGTON

STOWE

Winooski

Shelburne Farms

MONTPELIER

VERMONT

Vermont State House

NEW YORK

Otter Creek

White

Quechee Gorge Village

NEW HAMPSHIRE

New England Maple Museum

Green Mountains

Connecticut

RUTLAND

Green Mountain National Forest

SPRINGFIELD

Eureka Schoolhouse

Stellafane Observatory National Historic Landmark

7530

West

Bennington Battle Monument

BENNINGTON

BRATTLEBORO

MASSACHUSETTS

N W E S

0 — 20
Miles

QUICK FACTS

State capital: Montpelier
Largest city: Burlington
Total area: 9,614 square miles (24,901 sq km)
Highest point: Mount Mansfield, 4,393 feet (1,340 m), located in Lamoille County
Lowest point: Lake Champlain at 95 feet (29 m)

SAPPY STATE

It takes 40 gallons of sap to make one gallon of maple syrup, and Vermont is the largest producer of maple syrup in the U.S. So it's fair to call the state "sappy."

SKI GENIUS

Bunny Bertram of Woodstock developed the first motorized rope-tow ski lift in 1934. His stroke of genius? To power the lift using a Model T Ford engine.

ROAD TRIP!

In 1903, Dr. Horatio Nelson Jackson of Burlington became the first person to drive a car across the country. He traveled with Bud, his goggle-wearing bulldog, in a car named *Vermont*.

WHAT A HEADACHE

A plaque for Phineas Gage can be found in Cavendish. The railroad blaster suffered a metal rod driven through his skull in 1848. Not only did he survive, he never lost consciousness!

THE SNOWFLAKE MAN

Photographer Wilson A. Bentley became known as "the snowflake man" when he photographed a single snowflake in 1885. He went on to photograph 5,000, proving that no two snowflakes are alike!

AHEAD OF THE CURVE

Vermont was the first place in the nation to outlaw slavery. It was written into the original Constitution in 1777, before statehood, when Vermont was known as the Vermont Republic.

ESCAPE TO VERMONT

The Von Trapp family, featured in the musical and film *The Sound of Music*, settled in Stowe and opened the Trapp Family Lodge after escaping Austria during World War II.

ICE CREAM PIGS

Reportedly unused ice cream from the Ben & Jerry's factory in Waterbury goes to local pigs—except for one now-retired flavor. They turned up their noses at Mint Oreo Cookie.

MONSTROUS COUSINS

The Loch Ness Monster has a "cousin" who lives in Lake Champlain. Locals have named the beast Champ, who was first sighted in 1609 by explorer Samuel de Champlain.

WHALE OF A TALE

In 1849, some very puzzled railroad workers found a whale fossil in Charlotte. What was a whale doing in Vermont? During the ice age, Vermont was basically underwater.

N W E S

0 50
Miles

OHIO

PENNSYLVANIA

Arlington National Cemetery

Assateague Island National Seashore

N.J.

WEST VIRGINIA

Shenandoah Valley Caverns

Mount Vernon Estate and Gardens

MARYLAND

Washington, D.C.

ARLINGTON

DELAWARE

Monticello

CHARLOTTESVILLE

Edgar Allan Poe Museum

Pamunkey Indian Museum

Mountains

Shenandoah

Potomac

Chesapeake Bay

KENTUCKY

Black History Museum and Cultural Center

VIRGINIA

RICHMOND

Appalachian

ROANOKE

Virginia State Capitol

James

NEWPORT NEWS

NORFOLK

PJ's Carousel Collection

Roanoke

Yorktown Victory Center

VIRGINIA BEACH

Booker T. Washington National Monument

Historical Appomattox Court House National Historic Park

TENNESSEE

Jamestown Settlement

Great Dismal Swamp National Wildlife Refuge

NORTH CAROLINA

SOUTH CAROLINA

ATLANTIC OCEAN

QUICK FACTS

State capital: Richmond
Largest city: Virginia Beach
Total area: 42,774 square miles
  (110,784 sq km)
Highest point: Mount Rogers at
  5,722 feet (1,744 m)
Lowest point: Sea level along
  the Atlantic Ocean

SONGBIRD SMITH

Singer Kate Smith, whose famous recording of "God Bless America" is often heard at Yankee Stadium during the 7th inning stretch, was born in Greenville in 1907.

WORLD'S BIGGEST OFFICE

Arlington is home to the world's largest office building: the Pentagon, also known as the Department of Defense. It has 3.7 million square feet of space, and over 23,000 employees!

ESPIONAGE QUEEN

Elizabeth "Crazy Bet" Van Lew of Richmond ran a 12-person spy ring for the Union during the Civil War. The great spy is in the Military Intelligence Hall of Fame.

ROCK MUSIC

The Luray Caverns in Luray are a series of caves full of stalactites and stalagmites, including the Great Stalacpipe Organ, a musical instrument formed out of stalactites in the cave.

BACKWARD BOJANGLES

Richmond's Bill "Bojangles" Robinson, a famous tap dancer and film star, set a world record for running backward, completing a 75-yard backward dash in 8.2 seconds.

A BUSY WOMAN!

Lucy Diggs Slowe of Berryville established the first junior high school in Washington, D.C., and in 1917 became the first African American woman to win the American Tennis Association tournament.

GOD OF THE SEA

Virginia Beach welcomes its visitors with a 34-foot-tall statue of Neptune, the Roman god of the sea. He is accompanied by two dolphins, a loggerhead turtle, and an octopus.

GORY WARNING

Virginia authorities, tired of thieving pirates, hung Blackbeard's skull at the meeting point of the Hampton and James rivers, which is now known as Blackbeard Point.

ODD COINCIDENCE

Thomas Jefferson, author of the Declaration of Independence, was born in Shadwell in 1743. The founding father died 83 years later on the 4th of July, the document's 50th anniversary.

LAND OF PEACE

Two wars ended in Virginia. The Revolutionary War ended with the Battle of Yorktown in 1781 and the Civil War ended at the Appomattox Court House in 1865.

VIRGINIA

THE OLD DOMINION STATE

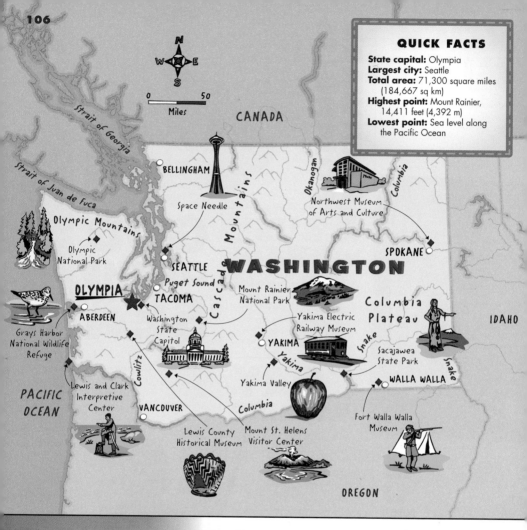

N W E S

0   50
Miles

CANADA

Strait of Georgia

Strait of Juan de Fuca

BELLINGHAM

Space Needle

Olympic Mountains

Olympic National Park

Okanogan

Northwest Museum of Arts and Culture

Columbia

SPOKANE

SEATTLE

WASHINGTON

Cascade Mountains

Puget Sound

TACOMA

OLYMPIA

ABERDEEN

Grays Harbor National Wildlife Refuge

Washington State Capitol

Mount Rainier National Park

Yakima Electric Railway Museum

Columbia Plateau

Snake

Sacajawea State Park

Snake

IDAHO

YAKIMA

Yakima

Yakima Valley

Cowlitz

Lewis and Clark Interpretive Center

PACIFIC OCEAN

VANCOUVER

Columbia

Lewis County Historical Museum

Mount St. Helens Visitor Center

WALLA WALLA

Fort Walla Walla Museum

OREGON

EARTHQUAKES AND VOLCANOES

In 1980, an earthquake caused the north face of the active volcano Mount St. Helens to collapse. Dust and ash spewed into the sky and blocked out the sun for days.

GEORGE, WASHINGTON

There is a town in Washington named George. This of course means that the last line of envelopes addressed to the city's residents says, "George, Washington"!

WEIRD GEOGRAPHY

If you're planning to travel to Point Roberts from any place in the U.S., bring your passport. In order to get to the U.S. town by car, you must pass through Canada!

ELECTRIFYING RIVER

The Grand Coulee Dam on the Columbia River is the greatest source of electricity in the United States. It provides one third of America's hydroelectric power!

WORLD FAMOUS BOB'S JAVA JIVE

JAVA JIVE

A 25-foot-high coffee pot built in Tacoma in 1927 is not only still standing, but it has been home to Bob's Java Jive—a coffee shop, bar, and music venue—since 1955.

In Everett, it is illegal for a hypnotist to display a hypnotized person in a store window for advertising purposes. The penalty is a $500 fine and up to six months in jail!

HYPNOTISTS, BEWARE!

WORLD'S OLDEST CELEBRITY

The Kennewick Man is a 9,300-year-old skeleton that was discovered by visitors watching hydroplane races in 1996 along the Columbia River. It's one of the oldest skeletons ever found in the Americas.

GOOEY DUCKS

Geoducks, pronounced "gooey ducks," are giant clams that can weigh up to 10 pounds, sporting 9-inch shells. These monstrous "ducks" can be found on Washington's Pacific coast.

GALLOPING GERTIE

The Tacoma Narrows Bridge, which was over a mile long and 39 feet wide, swayed so violently that locals called it "Galloping Gertie." It collapsed four months after opening in 1940.

STINKY FOREST

At 7,470 acres, the Ginkgo Petrified Forest near Kittitas is possibly the largest of its kind in the world. (Hopefully petrified ginkgo trees aren't nearly as stinky as non-petrified ginkgo trees!)

WASHINGTON

THE EVERGREEN STATE

MARYLAND

BETHESDA

SILVER SPRING

MARYLAND

Potomac

Rock Creek

Dalecarlia Reservoir

DISTRICT OF COLUMBIA

McMillan Reservoir

Georgetown University

Lincoln Memorial

ARLINGTON

Arlington National Cemetery

The Pentagon

VIRGINIA

Potomac

ALEXANDRIA

African American Civil War Memorial

U.S. National Arboretum

Anacostia

International Spy Museum

★ WASHINGTON, D.C.

Emancipation Statue

U.S. Capitol

Oxon Run

Frederick Douglass National Historic Site

MARYLAND

N
W E
S

0   2
Miles

QUICK FACTS

Total area: 68 square miles (177 sq km)
Highest point: Tenleytown at the Reno Reservoir, 410 feet (125 m)
Lowest point: Potomac River at sea level

WORLD TRAVELER

During Eleanor Roosevelt's first year as First Lady, she logged 38,000 miles of domestic travel. She was later given the title "First Lady of the World."

BAZILLIONS OF BOOKS!

The Library of Congress is the world's largest library, with over 120 million items! Every day, 22,000 new items arrive and 10,000 become part of the permanent collection.

PANDA-MONIUM!

Some of America's most powerful celebrities live in D.C., but no one draws more crowds on a daily basis than Tian Tian and Mei Xiang, the giant pandas at the National Zoo!

E = MC²

The Einstein Memorial on the grounds of the National Academy of Sciences depicts Einstein holding a piece of paper containing three equations summarizing the genius's greatest contributions to science.

WASHINGTON'S CHERRY TREES

In 1912, Japan gave 3,020 cherry trees to Washington. First Lady Helen Taft planted the first tree in a ceremony that inspired what has become Washington's annual Cherry Blossom Festival.

MODEST GEORGE

President George Washington did not like calling the nation's capital "Washington," so he called it the "Federal City" instead. Our first president was very modest!

THE DUKE

Duke Ellington, who began playing piano at age seven, was a brilliant bandleader from D.C. who won countless Grammy Awards and was posthumously recognized by the Pulitzer Prize committee.

COLOSSAL COLUMNS

The National Building Museum has some of the world's largest Corinthian columns (columns with a fluted shape and ornate designs at the top). They are 75 feet tall and 8 feet across.

ROGUE CITY

Washington, D.C., is the only city in the U.S. that is not part of a state. It is regulated by the federal government and officially called the "District of Columbia."

FUN WITH POLITICS!

Appropriately, Stephen Colbert, political satirist and hilarious host of Comedy Central's The Colbert Report, was born in Washington, D.C., in 1964. Must have been something in the water...

PENNSYLVANIA

WEIRTON

WHEELING

Prabhupada's Palace of Gold

International Mother's Day Shrine

Harpers Ferry National Historical Park

OHIO

MORGANTOWN

Berdine's Five and Dime

MARYLAND

MARTINSBURG

PARKERSBURG

Monongahela

Cheat

South Branch Potomac

Potomac

Mothman Museum and Research Center

Little Kanawha

Blackwater Falls State Park

WEST VIRGINIA

Kanawha

West Virginia State Capitol

Elk

Allegheny Mountains

Spruce Knob

Shenandoah

Washington, D.C.

Smoke Hole Caverns

Ohio

★ **CHARLESTON**

VIRGINIA

TINGTON

Mystery Hole

Gauley

National Radio Astronomy Observatory

Guyandotte

New River Gorge

New

Greenbrier

RoadKill Cook-off

BLUEFIELD

Lewisburg National Historic District

VIRGINIA

QUICK FACTS

State capital: Charleston
Largest city: Charleston
Total area: 24,230 square miles (62,755 sq km)
Highest point: Spruce Knob, 4,863 feet (1,482 m)
Lowest point: Potomac River, 240 feet (73 m)

TRAVELING IN STYLE

Students at West Virginia University in Morgantown travel their campus by train! The Personal Rapid Transit, or PRT, carries 15,000 people per day during the school year.

OLD NEW RIVER

The New River is thought to be the oldest river in North America. Unlike most rivers, the New River flows south to north, possibly because it was there before the rest of the landscape!

POWER SHIFT

During the Civil War, the strategically located city of Romney is said to have changed hands between the Union army and the Confederate army a whopping 56 times!

CAPITAL CRAZINESS

In 1863, West Virginia's capital was Wheeling. Then it was officially moved to Charleston, then back to Wheeling. Finally, in 1877, West Virginians voted and they chose Charleston. (Got that?)

WEST VIRGINIA

THE PERFECT LIE

Charleston's Vandalia Gathering has three types of competition each May: one for bakers, one for musicians—and one for liars. Storytellers compete to see who can tell the biggest lie!

THANKS, MR. PRESIDENT

West Virginia is the only state whose statehood was proclaimed by the president. Abraham Lincoln declared West Virginia's statehood in 1863, with the understanding that it would stop practicing slavery.

DOME COMPETITION

The capitol building in Charleston has the tallest dome of all the state capitols. At 293 feet, the dome is 5 feet taller than the capitol dome in Washington, D.C.

LITERACY LAWS

In 1835, three men and one woman in Wheeling were charged with a bizarre crime: teaching African Americans to read. At that time, it was illegal to educate slaves.

FAMOUS FEUD

The Hatfields and McCoys lived on opposite sides of the Tug Fork River, and fought a legendary feud over everything—the Civil War, women, even pigs—for 20 years.

PEEK AT PRISON

Curious about life behind bars? Visit Moundsville and take the State Penitentiary Tour. The prison was closed in 1995, but now serves to give people a true taste of lockup.

WEST VIRGINIA

THE MOUNTAIN STATE

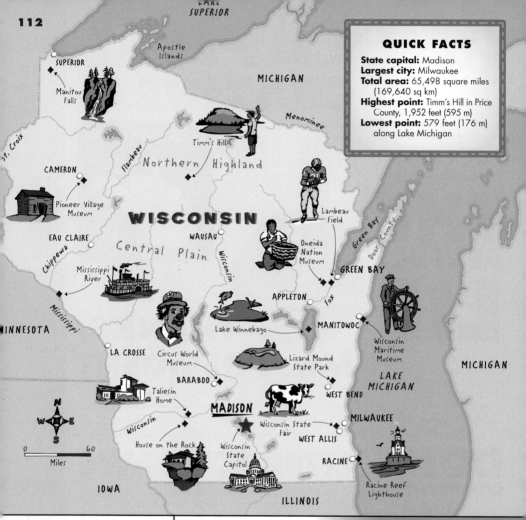

QUICK FACTS

State capital: Madison
Largest city: Milwaukee
Total area: 65,498 square miles (169,640 sq km)
Highest point: Timm's Hill in Price County, 1,952 feet (595 m)
Lowest point: 579 feet (176 m) along Lake Michigan

LAKE SUPERIOR

Apostle Islands

SUPERIOR

Manitou Falls

MICHIGAN

Menominee

Timm's Hill

St. Croix

CAMERON

Flambeau

Northern Highland

Pioneer Village Museum

WISCONSIN

WAUSAU

Lambeau Field

EAU CLAIRE

Central Plain

Wisconsin

Oneida Nation Museum

Green Bay

Door County

GREEN BAY

Chippewa

Mississippi River

Wisconsin

APPLETON

Fox

MANITOWOC

Wisconsin Maritime Museum

MINNESOTA

Mississippi

LA CROSSE

Circus World Museum

Lake Winnebago

Lizard Mound State Park

MICHIGAN

LAKE MICHIGAN

BARABOO

Taliesin Home

WEST BEND

N
W   E
S

0   60
Miles

Wisconsin

House on the Rock

MADISON

Wisconsin State Capitol

Wisconsin State Fair

WEST ALLIS

MILWAUKEE

RACINE

Racine Reef Lighthouse

IOWA

ILLINOIS

RIDDLES RACES

In 1985, Madison's Libby Riddles became the first woman to win Alaska's famous dogsled race, the Iditarod, which won her a place in the Iditarod Hall of Fame.

THE GIANT "MUSKIE"

Hayward hosts a giant muskellunge, which is half a block long, and four and a half stories high. It's considered the highlight of the National Freshwater Fishing Hall of Fame.

ENAMEL TRANSFORMATION

In 1883, John Michael Kohler of Sheboygan coated a pigs' watering trough with enamel, and realized that he'd just made the Kohler Company's first bathtub. So he sold it!

THE BADGER STATE

Wisconsin is the Badger State. In the 1830s, Wisconsin lead miners lived in hillside caves resembling badger dens, and the miners were known as badgers. The name stuck!

EARTH DAY INITIATOR

Long before it was cool to care about the environment, Senator Gaylord Nelson of Clear Lake lobbied for a national day of awareness. The first Earth Day was celebrated on April 22, 1970.

JUMP FOR JOY!

Bloomer, the "Rope Jump Capital of the World," hosts an annual speed jump rope contest for students in grades one through eight. The finals are held each year in January.

HOUDINI'S HOME

Ehrich Weiss, also known as "The Great Houdini," grew up in Appleton. The "master of mystery," who set the bar for magicians everywhere, is considered the world's best escapologist.

FEROCIOUS FIRE

Though the Great Chicago Fire grabbed all the headlines in 1871, an even more devastating fire ripped through the forests of Peshtigo on the same day, killing thousands.

ELEPHANTS ON PARADE!

Milwaukee's Great Circus Parade strolls for three miles through the town with over 75 vintage circus wagons, hundreds of horses, and yes, lots of elephants.

SUPER BOWL HISTORY

The Green Bay Packers won the first Super Bowl in American history held in Los Angeles in 1967. Coach Vince Lombardi's team slammed the Kansas City Chiefs, 35–10.

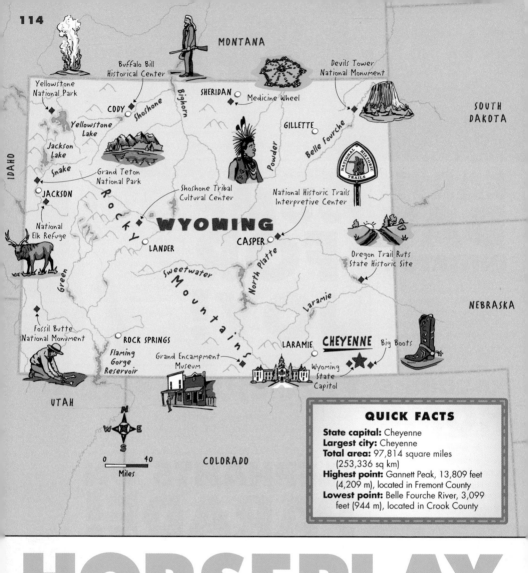

MONTANA

Buffalo Bill Historical Center

Devils Tower National Monument

SOUTH DAKOTA

Yellowstone National Park

SHERIDAN

Medicine Wheel

CODY   Shoshone

Bighorn

Yellowstone Lake

GILLETTE

Belle Fourche

NATIONAL HISTORIC TRAILS

Jackson Lake

Snake

Powder

Grand Teton National Park

IDAHO

JACKSON

Rocky

Shoshone Tribal Cultural Center

National Historic Trails Interpretive Center

WYOMING

National Elk Refuge

LANDER

CASPER

Oregon Trail Ruts State Historic Site

Sweetwater

North Platte

Green

Mountains

Laramie

NEBRASKA

Fossil Butte National Monument

ROCK SPRINGS

Flaming Gorge Reservoir

Grand Encampment Museum

LARAMIE CHEYENNE Big Boots

Wyoming State Capitol

UTAH

N
W   E
S

0   40
Miles

COLORADO

QUICK FACTS

State capital: Cheyenne
Largest city: Cheyenne
Total area: 97,814 square miles (253,336 sq km)
Highest point: Gannett Peak, 13,809 feet (4,209 m), located in Fremont County
Lowest point: Belle Fourche River, 3,099 feet (944 m), located in Crook County

HORSEPLAY

The bucking bronco on the Wyoming license plate is Steamboat, a legendary horse who refused to be ridden, bucking off the best rodeo riders of the early 20th century.

WYOMING IN SPACE

When the *Voyager* was sent into space in 1977, it contained a photograph of Jackson Hole by the famous photographer Ansel Adams—just in case there is anyone out there.

NO SWIMMING!

Don't ever go swimming in the beautiful blue Morning Glory Pool in Yellowstone National Park. You might dissolve as a result of the pool's high acidity. Ouch!

RODEO BUCKS

In Wyoming, you don't have to be a football player to get an athletic scholarship. The National Intercollegiate Rodeo Association offers scholarships to top rodeo athletes!

BIG BEAR!

Devil's Tower, the national monument featured in *Close Encounters of the Third Kind*, has a striped surface that Sioux legend says was caused by a bear clawing at the sides.

LEGEND OR REALITY?

The jackalope is a beloved creature in Wyoming—to those who believe it exists, anyway. The antlered rabbit is said to be able to run at close to 90 miles per hour. (Hmmm . . .)

PENNEY'S PENNIES

James Cash Penney bought the Golden Rule Store in Kemmerer in 1902, changed the name to JC Penney, and started down the path to riches and success!

CEMENT CAKES!

Nearly 40,000 people come to the free pancake breakfasts during the 10-day rodeo Cheyenne Frontier Days. The demand for pancakes is so great, the batter is sometimes mixed in cement trucks.

AHEAD OF THE GAME

Wyoming women were the first in the nation to be given the right to vote. In fact, they had the right to vote as soon as the Wyoming Territory was formed, in 1869.

DUDE, WHERE'S MY RANCH?

Crossed Sabres Ranch was the first dude ranch in Wyoming. Legend has it that the term "dude" referred to easterners who wanted to vacation on a ranch.

WYOMING

THE COWBOY STATE

Congratulations to the contest winners (listed below) and thanks to all the contributors!

Elizabeth Moreau, AK
Lisa Churchill, AL
Karen Scott, AL
Melisa Rutherford, AR
Melissa Wilson, AR
Michele Harbour, AZ
Brandee MacLean, AZ
Stephanie Ghinn, CA
Shannon Hunsinger, CA
Cindi Bryant, CO
Diane Webster, CO
Lisa Plavin, CT
Susan Ritter, CT
Barbara Miller, DC
Donna Reed, DE
Louisa Romaine, DE
Joan Molozaiy, FL
Marie Valletta, FL
Patricia Tucker, GA
Elaine Walker, GA
Carolyn Kirio, HI
Sandra Ongie, HI
Karol Dudley, IA
Joy Stoker-Hadow, IA
Lara Alexander, ID
Janice Simon, ID
Kathy Hempel, IL
April Johns, IL
Agnes George, IN
Roberta Kobbe, KS
Marcia O'Grady, KS
Prestine Chapman, KY
Suzanne Jameson, LA
Mia Orgeron, LA
Lyn Holian, MA
Cathy Rosenstock, MA
Paula Borinsky, MD
Richard Parker, MD
Jacquie Sewell, MI
Patricia Thunell, MI
Susan Boulka, MN
Elena Williams, MN
Diane Burger, MO
Cherie LeMay, MO
Jackie Jernigan, MS

Jean Bardwell, MT
LouAnne Krantz, MT
Holly Pierce, NC
Cindy Struth, NC
Susan Kempel, ND
Karen Retzlaff, ND
Paula Ashford, NE
Beth Foulks, NE
Nancy Polito, NH
Lesley Unger-Mochrie, NH
Alice DiNizo, NJ
Lynn Hotz, NJ
Kathy Barco, NM
Marla Layman, NM
Mary Jo King, NV
Shannon Broderick, NY
Nancy Williams, NY
Mary Gresco, OH
Sharon Touchton, OH
Mary Green, OK
Carolyn Gutierrez, OK
Renee Allen, OR
Julianne Brinker, OR
Barbara Flynn, PA
Gail McDonald, PA
Susan Baxter, RI
Lu Bickley, SC
Jan Dandridge, SC
Nancy Allee, TN
Lynnette Poston, TN
Shangruti Desai, TX
Peggy Shaw, TX
Susan Huff, UT
Beverly Stout, UT
Genevieve Gallagher, VA
Joyce Nelson, VA
Martha Allen, VT
Cheryl Cox, VT
Deborah Allen, WA
Kaylene Flanary, WA
Anita Folgert, WI
Ann Salt, WI
Pamela Mann, WV
Holly Baker, WY
Mary Wegher, WY